"I love this book! Backed up by extensive research, it gives the reader seven clear principles for a structured approach to understanding themselves and helping them to grow a high performance culture. Simply put, it will enable the reader to release new potential in their organization. *Work That Works* certainly works for me!"

—**Kosta Christofi, Senior Learning Manager, Santander, UK**

"The impact of language in the workplace is nothing short of amazing! When my team started to share the common language of Emergenetics, the entire atmosphere changed. People are showing greater consideration by being more inclusive of various personality types and more open to different perspectives and communication styles. The ability to Emergineer such positivity has served as a guiding light for all of us."

—**Sherrye L. Hutcherson, Vice President of Human Resources, Union Pacific Railroad**

"Few things are as vital to leadership, success and overall fulfilment as self-awareness and the ability to communicate precisely and honestly. *Work that Works* exquisitely shows you how on both accounts. With its bullseye principles, this treasure of a book is a homerun for individuals and organizations that want to be a major contender in this ferociously competitive world. I'd be surprised if you don't find at least three things in this book that transform you positively. Forever."

—**Scott G. Halford, *Wall Street Journal* bestselling author of *Activate Your Brain*, member of the National Speakers Hall of Fame, and Principal, Complete Intelligence, Inc.**

"Business books are typically written with good research and deep cognitive efforts. They speak to the head. *Work That Works*, a second book from Dr Geil Browning did not just score well in this area; this book speaks to the heart, mind and soul. Brought to life with her years of experience creating and using Emergenetics throughout her life, Geil's masterpiece will allow you to emergineer a truly positive corporate culture and a changed organization."

—**Josh Teo, Entrepreneur and Co-founder, Emergenetics APAC, Singapore**

"Dr. Geil Browning has been an inspiration to so many as she researched and created Emergenetics, founded ICAN (Institute for Career Advancement Needs) and has now developed Emergineering. As today's leaders grapple with the future of business, holding the interest of millennials and igniting profits, Emergineering is a key tool to understanding your team, growing your business and doing good in the communities where you employ people."

—**Susan L. Henricks, President and CEO, ICAN**

"Leaders who value, and wish to nurture, their human capital will find an incredible resource in *Work that Works*. This book reminds us to seek out the irreplaceable contributions of the individual and prompts us to deliberately tap into the magic of diverse teams. *Work that Works* is practical and structured. It will become your go-to handbook for creating a company that works."

—**Marty Lassen, Principal, Complete Intelligence, LLC**

"As I have been 'embracing the scratchy' since first bringing Emergenetics to U.S. Federal Government employees and their contractors in 2014, I found *Work That Works* an absolutely fabulous resource for the pragmatic application of Emergenetics and for fully developing the Power of We. *Work That Works'* eminent practicality made me wish I'd had all the templates and ideas when I had started! Bravo, Geil, and thank you for producing a succinct and powerful aid for us Emergineers!"

—**Gibson Kerr, Professor of Executive Acquisition Management, Defense Systems Management College, Defense Acquisition University**

"Our understanding of how human brains function effectively, means that successful future leaders and organizations need to rewire habits of where they spend their time and energy… every day… every meeting… every conversation. This book guides you in that quest. You will thoroughly enjoy the journey and reap the rewards. Your organization will become sustainable and transformed. Emergineer the future!"

—**David Sales, Executive Director, First Ascent Group, UK**

"After reading *Work That Works*, I formed a wholly new perspective on the importance of self-awareness. The knowledge of my preferences allowed me to renew my approach as a leader. I am empowered to Emergineer my approach in a way that will best serve those around me and the world we live in."

—**Regina Andreu, President, Latin Top Jobs, El Salvador**

work
that
works

Geil Browning, Ph.D.

work that works

An Emergenetics Guide

Emergineering
a Positive Organizational Culture

Our business model includes making sure each employee is understood, valued, engaged, and as healthy and productive as possible.

WILEY

Cover Design: Wiley
Cover Image: background © Gile68/iStock.com
Cover Illustration: © Tom Fishburne

All cartoons are created by Tom Fishburne at Marketoonist, and owned by Emergenetics

For general information about our other products and services, please contact our Customer Care Department within the United States at (800) 762-2974, outside the United States at (317) 572-3993 or fax (317) 572-4002.

Wiley publishes in a variety of print and electronic formats and by print-on-demand. Some material included with standard print versions of this book may not be included in e-books or in print-on-demand. If this book refers to media such as a CD or DVD that is not included in the version you purchased, you may download this material at http://booksupport.wiley.com. For more information about Wiley products, visit www.wiley.com.

Library of Congress Cataloging-in-Publication Data

Names: Browning, Geil, author.
Title: Work that works : emergineering a positive organizational culture / by
  Geil Browning, Ph.D.
Description: Hoboken, New Jersey : John Wiley & Sons, Inc., [2018] | Includes
  bibliographical references and index. |
Identifiers: LCCN 2017036478 (print) | ISBN 9781119387022 (cloth)
Subjects: LCSH: Leadership. | Organizational behavior. | Corporate culture.
Classification: LCC HD57.7 .B7697 2018 (print) | DDC 658.4/092–dc23
LC record available at https://lccn.loc.gov/2017036478

Printed in the United States of America

10 9 8 7 6 5 4 3 2

To Morgan, the Emergenetics staff, and Associates for pioneering Emergineering.

and

To Armistead, Tyler, and Ryan, who have been part of Emergenetics since its inception.

CONTENTS

Principle #7
LOVE   153
Care for Your People and the Profits Will Come

Conclusion and Acknowledgments   171

Appendix   175

Glossary of Emergenetics Terms   181

Sources   187

Emergenetics Templates
*At the end of each chapter, you will find supplementary
information in a graphic form, which we call the Emergenetics
Template. It is a method employed by Emergenetics to ensure
that any given process honors the four thinking and three
behavior Attributes.*

Index   191

FOREWORD

In the beginning, Emergenetics started as a tool that helped people decipher how they thought and behaved. It brought scientific objectivity to a most perplexing challenge: human behavior. People have characteristics that *emerge* from their life experiences, as well as factors that are hardwired by their *genetics*. The Emergenetics system introduced a simple, but not simplistic, framework that showed people how they naturally used their mental energies and how they presented themselves to the world. The Emergenetics Profile could be used by everyone to understand not only themselves but also their colleagues.

Since that time, we have seen Emergenetics evolve into a complete, scalable driver of positive change and systemic culture. The Profile still shows individuals how to prize their talents, but we also have learned so much more about helping people flex their attributes so they can perform in a well-rounded way and meet others with different preferences where they are. In addition, we have become more sophisticated at valuing and leveraging the talents of all employees in the workplace. We found out that *anything* can be interpreted by using an Emergenetics Profile, from brainstorming all aspects of a new project to buying a new home.

This book is written to help guide all levels of an organization to create a positive and productive working environment. When we stopped to look at our own offices and our own corporate climate, we realized that we had instinctively used Emergenetics priorities to guide our decisions, whether we were determining what colors to paint our walls or how to infuse our work, and our workplace, with our core values. In short, we had *Emergineered* our own organization.

Emergineering is the process of taking goals – such as building trust, preparing for the future, spurring innovation, and energizing workplace culture – and making sure every aspect of each goal reflects Emergenetics concepts. This results in a corporate climate that values and supports the most important asset of any organization: its people.

We use Emergineering to align an organization's culture and increase efficiency and productivity while fostering a climate of positivity and collaboration. The principles in this book are the culmination of over 25 years of research, data, and experience from our work with our clients as well as from our own growth. The seven principles in this book represent the best practices of Emergenetics, putting our concepts to their highest and best use.

Most organizations exist in a continuous process of transformation. Emergineering represents a company-wide approach to providing a consistent language to help people and teams work more effectively. This customizable process can fully support the vision and strategic goals of any business. Emergineering brings objectivity to difficult and subjective topics. An unwavering goal is to provide an environment in which individuals feel appreciated, heard, and unafraid. Ultimately, when people are happy in their jobs and believe their input contributes to the greater good of the company, the corporate culture becomes a key driver of business results!

Morgan Browning
President
Emergenetics International

WHAT IS EMERGINEERING, AND HOW WILL IT MAKE A DIFFERENCE TO YOU?

On December 9, 2008, our largest client placed a very large order for Emergenetics training within their company. I was excited and told my staff that we might even skip the financial crisis that was facing the country.

I was wrong. Two weeks later, the client called and canceled the order. By the end of the first quarter in 2009, we had lost 40% of our business.

For the preceding 16 years we had been helping organizations by using self-development seminars in which employees learned about their thinking and behavioral preferences. We helped them recognize how their individual attributes affected their lives, their work, and their team.

The name of our company, *Emergenetics*, comes from the fact that we are all the product of characteristics that *emerge* from our life experiences as well as attributes that are the result of our *genetics*. We successfully and scientifically determine each employee's unique attributes by scoring their answers to an Emergenetics survey. We also provide them with a personal color-coded Emergenetics Profile, which not only illustrates their preferences at a glance, but also compares their results to a global population (see the www.emergenetics.com for more information about the Emergenetics Profile or to review our Technical Report. You can also refer to my first book, *EMERGENETICS: Tap Into the New Science of Success*). Once individuals better understand themselves and share their Profiles with others, wonderful things happen.

After years of assessing hundreds of thousands of people, we proved that when organizations hire competent people, put the right Emergenetics teams together, and provide an Emergenetics culture, this results in increased innovation and productivity. Our seminars were met with great success. However, the financial crisis forced us to ask ourselves, "Is this only 'nice to know' information? How does Emergenetics make a difference when financial times get tough?"

As I was brainstorming with my team about where to go with the new economic reality, one person said, "Well, what do we do here in our office?"

IT WORKED FOR US, IT WORKS FOR OUR CLIENTS, AND IT WILL WORK FOR YOU

By the end of 2009, our business rebounded and we lost only 20% from 2008. We think that happened because companies got rid of their fat and decided to invest in training for their remaining leaders.

And we could help them. For the past seven years, we have made the Inc. 5000 list. In 2014, we were named one of Colorado's fastest-growing companies. We also continue to grow internationally because what works in Denver, Colorado, or New York City also works in Singapore or London or Cairo or Paris. I spend the majority of my time every year flying from our offices in Denver to destinations all over the world, speaking to prospective clients, visiting our Emergenetics offices in Ireland and Singapore, and visiting our representatives in the Americas, Africa, Asia-Pacific, Europe, and the Middle East. I have come to realize that languages and customs differ, but what makes people tick is the same all over the world. And the fact that people are people is great for growing our business.

The flip side is that in the United States employers and employees have the same issues.

- Fewer than one-third of employees love their jobs. They are referred to as *actively engaged*. The number has not improved for the last 15 years.

- One study found that 82% of workers do not trust their boss to tell the truth.
- Approximately 50% of workers just tolerate their jobs.
- Around 17% actively hate their jobs and will go out of their way to disrupt the work that is being done.
- A full 91% of workers said they switched jobs purposely to get away from their previous management.

These statistics show that many companies need to do things a lot better. To begin with, they need to understand the danger and cost of unhappy employees. Our business model at Emergenetics is to make sure each employee is understood, valued, engaged, and as healthy and productive as possible. How could we make companies recognize the value of Emergenetics in all their operations and decisions? How could we help them change their corporate cultures to fix rampant dissatisfaction?

WHAT MAKES EMERGENETICS UNUSUAL?

- Our approach is inclusive, diverse, and collaborative.
- We develop our employees based on their Emergenetics Profiles, encouraging them to work through their strengths to succeed.
- We make sure every presentation appeals to all types of individuals.
- We make sure every meeting is based on cognitive diversity.
- Collaboration and working in teams are part of our corporate culture.
- We value our colleagues and their unique gifts – not *even though* they are different from us but *because* they are different from us.
- Our company is a place where other people want to come to work because we do not emphasize conformity.
- We are dedicated to the professional progress of our employees.
- We promote engagement, loyalty, and enthusiasm.
- We place a priority on employee well-being.
- We maintain a global outlook.

- We shape the future instead of simply running into it.
- We embrace change, and accept that anticipating and managing change is part of work that works.
- We have our own nonjudgmental language – *the Language of Grace* – that everyone uses to ensure a positive working environment.
- We hire new people on the basis of our own Emergenetics Selection Profile (ESP), which evaluates who is most likely to succeed in an available position.
- When onboarding new employees, everyone shares their individual Emergenetics Profiles – both the new and current employees – to be transparent about how we think and behave.
- We acknowledge the ways in which we might improve.
- Our response to changing market conditions is creative, innovative, and agile.
- We recognize how all these components help the bottom line.

PASSION, PRODUCTIVITY, AND PROFITS INCREASE WITH HUMAN INTERACTION

Emergineering cannot be accomplished with memos from the corporate office. It even requires a deeper commitment than putting all your leaders in a room for one day of Emergenetics training. That's a good start, but it will take sustained commitment to create a new corporate culture.

If you resist some of these concepts, try to get out of your comfort zone – what we call *feeling scratchy* – long enough to give this guide your earnest effort. If you positively can't relate to any of these principles, pass this book on to someone else because you're not ready to grasp the way business is going to be in the future.

On the other hand, if you're curious about successfully Emergineering your team, department, or company, I encourage you to keep reading! As a CEO, manager, or direct report, you're in the best position to Emergineer your company into the future. This book is written for those exceptional leaders who will pass these principles on to their direct reports, who will pass them on to their direct reports, and so on, until every employee understands their new corporate culture in which everything is done with transparency, with intention, and without judgment for the benefit of all.

If you've been wondering about the best way to adapt your leadership to the future, hold the interest of millennials, and ignite profits, there's a new leadership coach in town: WORK THAT WORKS!

LEADERSHIP IS AN INSIDE JOB

Know Yourself

Thousands of articles and research papers have been written about leadership. This, the first principle, deals with *you* as a leader: your values, the ways in which you think and behave, and how these affect your actions and your communication with your employees.

Let's start with three universal questions:

1. Who are you?
2. What do you love?
3. How can you restore balance to a troubled world?

After you are able to answer these questions, you are ready to start reflecting on how to be a leader.

WHO ARE YOU?

We live in a world that is more transparent than ever. The Internet has afforded everyone unprecedented access to information that permits unlimited discoveries.

People are using this information for everything from checking out a rash to creating political movements. Using this window into the world, sophisticated users can research the most advanced studies and esoteric information, while even basic users have learned to research the goods and services they need before they pay up or sign up. Before going out to eat, they will check a restaurant's online reputation. If the reviews are bad, they will look in another direction. If the reviews are good, they will proceed with their research and find the menu.

Think of a large purchase you have made recently. I'm willing to bet that some of you obtained a variety of information about what you were buying ahead of time, that you located some options about where to buy it, and that you determined how much you could reasonably expect to pay based on a comparison of prices in your area or even nationally.

It's no surprise that prospective job candidates are doing the same thing. It's easier than ever to find out what's behind the curtain of a place to work. All manner of information is readily available online. Who runs the company and what are their backgrounds? Has the company been involved in any litigation? How does it treat its employees? How well are they compensated? What are the working conditions like? What benefits, such as healthcare, are available? Does the company support continuing education? Does it reach for a higher calling?

Similarly, it's every bit as easy to discover how different individuals lead. Bernie Madoff was able to con people out of billions of dollars because his investors *thought* they knew him. They did not check out his financials before they invested. If they had, it would have been easy for them to spot the very large, very red flags. Through the window of the Internet, the danger signs were hiding in plain sight.

Transparency is a key pillar of leadership. Today, leaders are in the public eye, and someone who takes the time to look will be able to find out a great deal about you. Have you considered what they will discover? Are you aware of how you portray yourself at the office? Do people feel that they really know who you are and what you stand for? Is your authenticity apparent in your leadership style?

Reasonable people don't expect leaders to be heroes. They would simply like to know that they can count on the leaders, that the leaders have their interests at heart and are taking care of the greater whole. They would like to be able to expect that when the sun rises in the morning, they will have a place to go to work. Ideally, this place of work promotes such virtues as honesty, accountability, respect, collaboration, trust, and concern for the future.

Since 1982, and together with two colleagues – Carol Hunter and Tim Rouse – I facilitated a repeating 12-day leadership development program that was presented over 9 months. It was sponsored by the Institute for Career Advancement Needs (ICAN). Initially, the stated goal was coaching leadership development for high potential executives. Ultimately, we figured out that we were helping them, and us, figure out who we are from *the inside out.*

Back then, companies had very little interest in engaging in these sorts of development opportunities. We would walk into an executive's office to pitch the idea, and many times we were greeted with blank stares, or responses like, "Who cares about other people's feelings? How does this help anybody do their job?" Some companies did buy into this idea, and a few were forced to do so through government regulations, so we were able to begin making a difference.

We started Influence as a women-only program at a time when women in the workforce were moving into leadership positions. Three successful years later, I was giving a presentation to the ICAN Board of Directors and the General Manager of the Western Electric Works in Omaha said, "If this program is so valuable, why don't you offer it for men?" In 1985, we started a companion program, Focus, for men.

Over the last 40 years or so, I've seen over 2,500 leaders of several generations come through Influence and Focus and rise through the ranks of their organizations. As they introduced themselves on the first day, each generation of leaders generally shared similar perspectives on their work lives.

- In the 1980s, these leaders, both women and men, would start by stating, "My name is Pat Smith and I work for XYZ organization."
- In the 1990s, they would say, "My name is Pat Smith, I work for XYZ corporation, and I'm married with two kids."
- In the 2000s, a noticeable shift began to happen. Now the introduction was, "My name is Pat Smith, my loves are my life partner, Chris; my children, Emily and Nathan; and Bart, our German Shepherd.... Oh, and I work at XYZ corporation."

Clearly, these high-potential leaders had begun viewing their lives outside of work as every bit as important, if not more important, than what was occurring inside the walls of work. This trend is prevalent across the working world (more on this in Principle #6: Let Your People Live to Work). My belief is that the same values that people expect out of their friends and loved ones (honesty, trustworthiness, genuine care, and concern) are creeping more and more into the workplace. As work continues to look like home, people are desiring these same characteristics from their leaders, and a company's value is seen less and less through its balance sheet. The traditional assets that make up a company's value (office space, machines, retail locations, reputation, visibility) are being replaced with the value of human capital, which cannot be directly quantified. Innovation, teamwork, productivity, and flexibility are the real assets that help corporations remain nimble through these turbulent times of business change.

Look at all the retailers that have failed recently, such as those that once operated the now-empty stores in malls. Chances are that these companies continued to use the old model of success, including brick-and-mortar stores with visibility and access to shoppers. They continued to move merchandise and put it on shelves, but paid little attention to their brand, their employees, or the typical shopper's experience. While they weren't looking, other businesses were building brand loyalty, investing in their people, and noticing that shoppers were going online and not to the mall. The accumulation of property was not able to save the traditional stores while their respective industries encountered tectonic shifts they were not prepared to handle.

The job of the leader is to harness the company's biggest yet undefinable asset – its human capital – and to usher its workers successfully through the changes occurring in society. It's up to you to notice what's happening in the real world and translate it into a vision for what's going to happen next, and how that will affect the people who work for you.

HOW WELL DO YOU KNOW YOURSELF?

What makes you uniquely qualified to lead? Why are you a leader and your neighbor someone who sells mattresses? What is it about your thought processes, your judgment, your behavior, and your relationships with people that makes you uniquely qualified to manage the livelihoods of dozens or hundreds or thousands of people? At the heart of your success is this principle of knowing yourself from the inside out.

We know ourselves through self-discovery, understanding our roots, examining our values and ethics, and realizing how we are – and are not – like others. We can't appreciate what other people have to offer until we identify how we're different. Ultimately, we must strive to understand how our actions create the problems that we experience. This kind of personal reflection is made faster and easier by using the Emergenetics Profile.

In Emergenetics, we have pinpointed three behavioral factors (**Expressiveness**, Assertiveness, and Flexibility) and four thinking factors (**Analytical**, Structural, **Social**, and Conceptual) that everyone possesses. The way each leader uses these behavioral and thinking factors is unique. With an Emergenetics Profile, anything is possible. That's the delight of this system. No one is put in a box with thousands of other people. You have your very own Profile because you are a precious snowflake. OK, that's a joke – but you *are* unique and so is your Profile.

If you have already taken an Emergenetics Profile, here is a review of the seven attributes. If you don't have your Profile at your fingertips, I recommend that you take it out now. If you have *not* taken a Profile, turn to the appendix, where there is a template with adjectives that can help you identify your preferences. Circle the adjectives that describe you, and this should help you understand your Emergenetics preferences. If you do not already have a Profile, be certain to use these pages! You will want to have an idea of your Profile as you read the rest of this book.

You may notice, particularly if you are an **Analytical** thinker, that there are 13 attributes when you count all the thirds of each behavioral attribute as separate factors (e.g., first-third Assertiveness, second-third Assertiveness, third-third Assertiveness). Also, you may be interested to know that all the Emergenetics instruments have gone through rigorous testing, following the *Standards for Educational and Psychological Testing*. (To find out more about this, please go to www.emergenetics.com to review the Technical Report.) The appendix also includes a Tour of the Profiles, which gives an illustration and description of each of the more common Profiles.

Now, armed with either your online Profile or your self-made Profile, read this short description of the attributes to familiarize yourself with them.

THE BEHAVIORIAL ATTRIBUTES

The behavioral attributes are scored as percentiles. That means your answers to the behavioral questions on the questionnaire were compared to those of everyone else in the global population. The scores range from 0 to 100 percentiles on three spectrums. We have found over the years that it is useful to group people by thirds.

The behavioral factors can be observed by other people. Remember that after you complete an online Emergenetics Questionnaire, each of your factors – based on your responses – is given a percentile. Behavioral attributes are divided into thirds:

- 33% of the population will fall in the first third (their scores are within the 0–33% percentile).
- 33% will fall in the second third (their scores are within the 34–66% percentile).
- 33% will fall in the third third (their scores are within the 67–100% percentile).

As you will read in Principle #3: The Language of Grace, we never describe the people on any part of the spectrum as missing something or having too much of something. They are fine the way they are. You will never see descriptions like not expressive, not assertive, or inflexible. Instead, we say quiet, peacekeeping, or focused. As a shortcut, we refer to the thirds: "She is first-third

Flexibility," or "He is third-third **Expressiveness**." Similarly, you will not see phrases like very expressive, aggressive, or wimpy. It takes a little getting used to, but intuitively it makes so much sense that soon you'll be saying "third third" and not even realizing it.

What happens to those in the second third? Thirty-three percent of the population can flex their attribute either way, depending on the circumstances. We call them the *It Depends* group.

1. First look at your **Expressiveness**. Are you more comfortable in one-on-one conversations or are you comfortable being on stage? Are you an internal processor or do ideas enter your head and go straight out of your mouth? Do you look to connect very deeply with just a few people or do you have many connections (both deep and shallow) with lots of people? If you answered yes to the first part of each question, chances are you are at the quiet, more internal end of the **Expressiveness** spectrum. Your strengths are that you take time to think before you speak; you probably listen well; and you have a composed, calm demeanor when faced with difficult challenges.

   Are you more gregarious and outgoing? You probably fall in the third third of Expressiveness. Many people may see you as exuberant and ebullient, even a show-off. Your strengths are that you are convincing and able to bring many people to the table.

2. Now check your **Assertiveness**. Leaders who are on the easy-going end of the **Assertiveness** spectrum tend to be have a calming presence and take the time to listen to others. The fact that they are not excitable should not be confused with the idea that they do not care. People at the first third of **Assertiveness** may care a great deal, but they don't run around like a house is on fire. **Assertiveness** is separate from **Expressiveness**. If your preference is to be a natural peacekeeper, don't be afraid to push your ideas. Most likely you will still operate in a respectful way, so no one will think you are being a bully.

   Leaders who are on the driving end of the **Assertiveness** spectrum approach their style with intensity. With this hard-charging approach you know exactly where they stand. If you're competitive and persistent, make sure you don't bowl over others, and try to respectfully build consensus.

3. Finally, check your Flexibility. How do you get things done? Your Flexibility determines not only how open-minded you are to other points of view but also your ability to thrive in undefined or changing situations. If your Flexibility is in the first third of the spectrum, you are most likely focused and firm. For you, change is difficult. Effective leaders recognize that change is constantly happening whether they welcome it or not. Uncertain situations like mergers, changing company-wide software, or large employee turnover can temporarily rock your routine – but *feeling scratchy* (see Principle #2: Embracing the *Scratchy*) is a healthy sign that you are learning, and that your company is accommodating the present and anticipating the future. To flex your Flexibility, go to your **Analytical** preference and remind yourself why a particular change is occurring and what wonderful effects it is going to have.

    If your Flexibility is in the third third of the spectrum, you most likely welcome change and are energized by having lots of options. You're probably accommodating and don't mind interruptions. Although it's fun for you to discuss everybody's ideas, the more focused members of your team may become frustrated. You can't put off making a decision forever, so eventually you'll have to just go for it.

THE THINKING ATTRIBUTES

The thinking attributes are measured in terms of your unique brain and how the different attributes relate to each other. In the case of the thinking attributes, the sum of your percentiles is converted into percentages in order to generate a pie chart. If a thinking attribute is 23% of your pie chart or more, it's considered a preference. (If a piece of your pie is at 22%, you're considered a near miss in that attribute.) You may have one to four thinking preferences at the same time.

SINGLE DOMINANT
ANALYTICAL

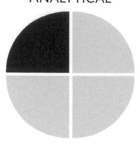

SAMPLE PROFILE

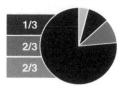

The **Analytical** attribute is logical, data-driven, and rational. It is the objective, factual part of the brain that asks why. A leader with a preference for **Analytical** thinking will want facts and measurements to inform everything the leader hears, says, and does. **Analytical** thinking is critical, skeptical and has a sound and deductive thought and reasoning process. It is not content with surface descriptions and wants to examine things in depth. This leader will expect the same kind of analysis and rigor from the workforce. The motto is, "In God we trust, all others must bring data." When I talk about the Analytical leaders, only 1% of the population is single dominant in this preference.

SINGLE DOMINANT
STRUCTURAL

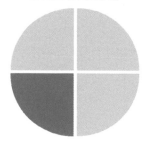

SAMPLE PROFILE

The Structural attribute is process-driven. It's the practical part of your brain that considers details, replicable guidelines, or frameworks. It likes rules, practicality, and any kind of sequential, numerical, or alphabetical order. It brings order to chaos and asks, "How can we get this done?" The motto is, "Of course I don't look busy, I did it right the first time." Only 6% of the population is single dominant in this preference. The rest are mixed with preferences of other attributes.

SINGLE DOMINANT
SOCIAL

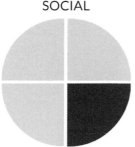

The Social attribute is collaborative, team-focused, and oriented toward relationships and a desire to get things done

SAMPLE PROFILE

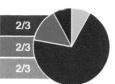

through people. People with this preference are able to connect ideas and work to the human element. They consult others to make a decision and also use gut instinct. The motto is, "I am intuitively aware of those around me." Only 1% of the population has this as a single dominant preference.

SINGLE DOMINANT
CONCEPTUAL

The Conceptual attribute prefers abstract ideas, imagination, innovation, and vision. This brain pathway has an intuitive

SAMPLE PROFILE

sense of the bigger picture, a proclivity for thinking about the long-term horizon, and a desire to experiment and invent new things. The motto is "I feel like I'm diagonally parked in a parallel universe." Just 2% of the population has this as a single dominant preference.

Each thinking attribute has its own unique combination of *abstract*, *concrete*, *convergent*, or *divergent* thought. In the illustration below, the top two thinking attributes are both abstract and the bottom two are both concrete. At the same time, the two thinking attributes on the left are both convergent, and the two on the right are divergent. Each thinking attribute is unique but also related to the other thinking attributes.

ABSTRACT, CONCRETE, CONVERGENT,
AND DIVERGENT THOUGHT

- *Abstract* thought sees systems and overviews. Abstract thinkers imagine a forest as if they were in an airplane looking down upon it.
- *Concrete* thought sees details and functionality. Concrete thinkers imagine they are walking through the forest and counting all the trees.
- *Convergent* thought prefers things in practical, rational order. It uses already proven facts and data to converge from what is known to find the correct answer.
- *Divergent* thought prefers intuition, emotion, synergy through people, and the unusual. It diverges from what is known to identify a unique solution.

YOUR LEADERSHIP PROFILE IS PERFECT THE WAY IT IS

In Emergenetics, there's no such thing as one perfect leadership Profile. And something that makes me crazy is any assertion that extroversion or a high degree of aggressiveness is important to be an effective leader. We have an Emergenetics Profile of a well-known CEO/entrepreneur whose behavioral preferences, when ranked against the global population, are quiet, affable, and firm. And we have many whose Profiles indicate that the energy around their behaviors is somewhere in the middle. We have the Profile of another well-known CEO whose behaviors are gregarious, driven, and accommodating.

Leadership is more than just knowing yourself, but it starts with embracing what that means. Knowing your particular thinking preferences means that you like to devote your energy to certain types of tasks. It also means you may accidentally-on-purpose overlook tasks associated with the thinking preferences that you do not have. Although you may not have a preference in a given attribute, it's not an excuse to disengage from those activities altogether. We have a slogan at Emergenetics: *no whining!* What we mean by that is, if you don't like your Profile, or if you think that you can ignore a particular attribute because it's not one of your preferences, you're mistaken. Lack of preference is not an excuse for nonperformance. Like reading a document without your prescription glasses, you can accomplish the task, but you just may have to strain and concentrate harder.

Part of being a leader is being transparent about your Profile. We live in a world in which we're expected to deliver results to achieve success, and we're constantly asked to operate outside of our preferences. A key step in ultimately being successful is knowing where our strengths lie and where we need others to help.

Jeff was the president of a Fortune 500 company. The company had utilized Emergenetics for over a year when he asked us to speak to him about the results of a survey given to his team that rated his performance. We of course agreed and reviewed both the questions and responses from the 25 participants. At

Emergenetics, it's a common practice of ours to filter survey responses such as these through the Emergenetics Template. For example, phrases such as "he really cares about people" are typically associated with a **Social** preference, or "he sticks to what was agreed upon" is considered a first-third Flexible trait. The survey responses become much more revealing and applicable when you arrange the information in this manner.

JEFF'S PROFILE

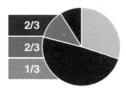

For Jeff, this definitely was the case. He's a **Social**/Conceptual thinker with second-third and first-third behaviors. Every piece of positive feedback that Jeff received from his colleagues reflected his Emergenetics profile. Phrases like "he gets me," "he has a great vision for the future," "he can see the bigger picture," "he is approachable," and "he knows when to speak and when to listen" are all positive reflections that are clearly associated with his Profile. On the other hand, all of the opportunities comments fell into the opposing attributes or where Jeff did not have a preference. We saw phrases like "he needs to send an agenda ahead of time," "he needs to support his points with more data," "his meetings tend to last three hours," and "sometimes we just need to make a decision and move on."

When we sorted the survey responses into the template and compared it to his Profile, Jeff had several Aha! moments as he realized that his natural tendencies were being subconsciously recognized by his team. Once his leadership qualities were on display, Jeff asked, "How do I shore up these areas they are identifying in these survey results, and how can I honor my team and get the most out of them through their Emergenetics preferences? Twenty-five people operating at peak performance is far greater than just me operating at a peak level."

TEAM PROFILE

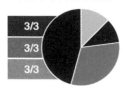

Jeff's executive group had a Team Profile that looked like this – the opposite of his in many ways. To satisfy his team's very different **Analytical**/Structural thinking preferences, as well as their behaviors, we crafted customized techniques for him to leverage the strengths of the others on his team so they would complement Jeff's preferences.

The key to this story is that Jeff was willing to accept this feedback with the seriousness that it deserves. Furthermore, the Emergenetics framework made it easy for him to categorize his people's words and define ways to address their concerns in the future.

Back in the 1980s, it would be much more common for the leader to take this same sort of feedback, and state, "It's not my problem, it's theirs! I'm the boss, and my team needs to tailor themselves to me." Kudos to Jeff!

WHAT DO YOU LOVE?

Do you love your work? Most successful people are attracted to work that energizes them, but that does not mean they work according to their preferences.

At one point, I attended a conference break-out session in which I was asked the question, "Do you love your job and why do you love it?" Then we were asked to go around the room and verbalize our responses.

As people went around the table, it struck me that there was intense pressure for people to answer in the way that they thought the others in the room wanted to hear. In other words, I actually heard a man say, "Yes, I love my job, because nothing gets me more excited than transporting asphalt by rail!"

While I pondered the truth of this particular statement, it caused me to reflect on what it was that I truly loved about my job. Did I love my job because of the traditional nature of my work, or was it something else that drove me, and the job was merely a vehicle to achieve this true passion? As you will see, the answer surprised me in many ways.

I encourage you to be true to yourself and ask in quiet reflection, "Do I love my job?" Regardless of the answer, I would invite you to explore why, or why not?

I bet this simple exercise will surprise you regarding what it reveals. You may say things like:

1. I love the company and what it stands for.
2. I believe in our mission.
3. I love helping people.
4. This job inspires my passion for numbers.
5. I get to play in uncharted waters.
6. We are on the forefront of technology.
7. I like to make things grow.
8. I like to maintain consistency.

Once you have explored this idea and come up with your reasons for loving work, I then would take it a step further and compare your answer to your Profile. Do your answers match what is reflected in the Profile? It may not always match, and that is okay. Regardless of the outcome, you will find some value in exploring why there is or isn't a perfect match.

This exercise brings clarity to your efforts and ultimately allows you to lead others to pursuing their own paths of work they love. Once a path is discussed with your direct reports, it will help you to help them pursue their passions within the framework of the company as a whole. The value of this cannot be overstated.

One time, I was debriefing the owner of an accounting firm on her particular Emergenetics results. I was shocked that her Profile revealed that she was a **Social**/Conceptual thinker and her behaviors were gregarious (**Expressiveness**), driven (Assertiveness), and fluid (Flexibility). This is not a Profile that you would expect from someone who spends the majority of her time crunching numbers, editing spreadsheets, and pouring over thousands of pages of U.S. tax code.

I asked her, "What do you love about being an accountant?" She told me that her greatest love was the fact that she was the entrepreneur of the company. "I enjoy helping people and coming up with creative (yet legal) solutions for my clients. In particular, I love looking at their faces when I present innovative solutions to solve their particular tax challenges."

I have worked with many accountants over the years, and many times they had the opposite Profile – quiet, amiable, and focused (**Analytical**/**Structural**). When I asked these folks what they love about what they do, I would hear responses such as "I love working with data," "I like to be a problem solver," "There is a logical conclusion to the work," "There is a predictability in the work." The work may be similar, but it is wonderful to hear people's unique passions come through their Profile.

What can we do to make a difference in the way people love to work? Bob Chapman has figured it out at his company, Barry-Wehmiller. You can read all about it in his bestseller, *Everybody Matters: The Extraordinary Power of Caring for Your People Like Family*. His company uses the word *stewardship* to describe its leadership approach.

> To us, stewardship means to truly care, to feel a deep sense of responsibility for the lives we touch through our leadership…. Stewardship implies accountability that goes beyond simple business ethic; it means acting from our deepest sense of right. Stewardship also implies trust and freedom of choice; we're not forcing or commanding followers, we're inspiring and guiding them. It is not about the exercise of power over another; it is an opportunity for service, an opportunity to exercise power through and with others in service to the greater good, to the shared vision and purpose of the organization, and to those in it…. We do everything we can to create an environment in which our people can realize their gifts, apply and develop their talents, and feel a genuine sense of fulfillment for their contributions. In other words, Barry-Wehmiller is in business to improve lives.

They are in the business of building capital equipment and offering engineering consulting! Bob loves his work. He cares about his employees, who enjoy coming to work, and they produce for Barry-Wehmiller as if they are part of the family.

As a manager, it's a great advantage for me to have this information so I can inspire and guide my folks to the things that bring them the most energy. And, when they are working within a job that they love, it rarely ever feels like a job.

Therefore, are you asking your employees this same question? Do you really know what your people love about their job, or are you getting responses they think you want to hear? Furthermore, can you see their responses in their Profiles?

Ultimately, this process may even lead you to the point where you hear the response "I am fascinated with moving asphalt by rail!"

HOW DO YOU RESTORE BALANCE TO A TROUBLED WORLD?

Restoring balance to a troubled world starts with restoring balance to yourself.

In 1999, my friend JoAnne LeClair invited me to travel to Kenya to join her in a nonprofit endeavor, which is now known as the Kenyan Girls Education Fund. Our goal was to provide transformational experiences to interested individuals who were willing to commit themselves to compassionate involvement with Kenyan children, many of whom are HIV-positive. The goal is not ecotourism for wealthy travelers but a longstanding commitment to a part of the world that has so little but can teach us so much.

Over the years, my spouse and I have made a trip to Kenya every two years, and we have brought groups of interested executives with us. At first, I thought the goal of our trips was to change the lives of the children in Kenya. What I quickly realized, however, was the goal of these trips was to change *my* life and the lives of those who came with us. It provided a chance for me to face my own shadows and ultimately bring balance to myself.

One executive who joined us is Matthew Wilson, Group Chief Executive Officer of Brit Insurance, based in London. He traveled to Nairobi, Kenya to check out the dormitory his company was supporting us to build. The dormitory was located in a school in Kibera, Africa's largest slum, adjacent to downtown Nairobi. The population exceeds over a million people. Wages are low; basic services such as electricity, running water, and sewer are in scarce supply.

In the evening, we all would gather to reflect on our experiences. During his reflection time, Matthew told the group that he was very proud of his business accomplishments, that he had quickly risen to great heights within the organization, and that he had worked very hard to make this happen. Yet, even though he was the CEO, he still was searching for purpose in his life and he was hoping his trip to Kenya would give him this opportunity.

As Matthew was checking out the new dorm, that opportunity occurred. He was looking at the existing facility, which was a converted classroom where 20 girls slept together in bunk beds, most of them sleeping two to a bed. On one of the beds, Matthew saw a pillow that stated, "LOVE YOU FOREVER."

Seeing this pillow struck him deeply. Despite these conditions, the girls were so thankful for their opportunity to have an education and safe domicile that they had adopted the mantra "LOVE YOU FOREVER."

Matthew left the room thinking about his own son, living in a very posh boarding school in Britain. Professionally, Matthew had conquered his own shadows and walked through many dark woods to get to his level of success. He had reached the mountaintop of his professional life, he knew all the Wharton School technical information, and now it was time to check into his heart before he could achieve his purpose in life.

I am sure that most of you contribute money to organizations, happily so, but have you, like Bob Chapman or Matthew Wilson, faced the moment when you figure out that power and money are only part of the equation?

Both Bob Chapman and Matthew Wilson crossed over multiple abysses to achieve their success. Their walk through the dark woods gave them compassion and empathy, which gave them balance that they did not learn at business school.

Many times, individuals believe that simply engaging in volunteer or nonprofit work is the key to restoring balance. Although I don't dispute the importance of this work, it's hard for people who are not in balance with themselves to bring balance to others. Matthew realized that his personal balance did not meet his professional balance, and he strove to change this.

In my opinion, inner balance is an important quality for leaders. Have you had the opportunity to face your fears and walk through the unknown? Have you seen the depths of your own abyss and yet still remained standing?

When you have accepted these challenges, others can sense it, and they will ask for your help in guiding them through their own challenges of the unknown.

After walking through this journey, the world seems less out of balance and not as threatening.

REFLECTION

Genuine leadership, or stewardship, is not possible without authenticity – and authenticity by definition cannot be faked. Employees are looking for leaders who do not pretend to know it all and who are comfortable with the fact that they are not superheroes. Leaders can, and should, be transparent about the fact that they have struggled through great challenges and ultimately persevered to achieve harmony and balance. They need to convey that they have learned to love who they are, warts and all; that they love what they spend their time doing; and that they are in balance with the world. The best leaders do not reflect any particular Emergenetics Profile, but they know how to use their strengths to achieve a level of inner peace and understanding that engages and inspires others to conquer their own challenges, not only professionally but also in their personal lives.

IMPLEMENTATION STEPS

1. Review your Emergenetics Profile (see the appendix if you still need to create one) and reflect on how it has made itself apparent in your life.
2. Ask yourself, what do you love about your job, and how does it show up in your Profile? Look at this chapter's templates and see how they match your Profile.
3. Identify which dark woods you face, and how you can walk through them to achieve balance.

TEMPLATES FOR PRINCIPLE #1:
LEADERSHIP IS AN INSIDE JOB

1. **WHAT KIND OF LEADER ARE YOU?**
   As a reality check, ask your team what they consider to be your leadership style.

2. **WHAT ARE YOUR STRENGTHS AS A LEADER?**
   As a reality check, ask your team what they consider to be your strengths.

3. **QUESTIONS TO ASK ABOUT YOUR COMPANY**
   What to consider about your company.

What Kind of Leader Are You?

As a reality check, ask your team what they consider to be your leadership style.

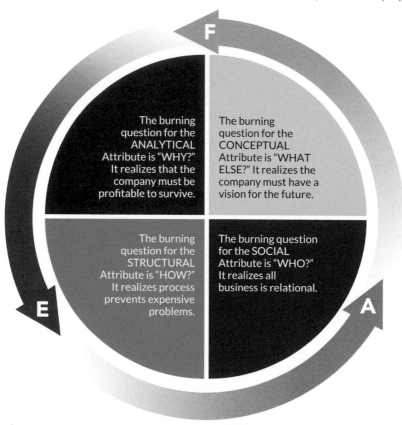

F

The burning question for the ANALYTICAL Attribute is "WHY?" It realizes that the company must be profitable to survive.

The burning question for the CONCEPTUAL Attribute is "WHAT ELSE?" It realizes the company must have a vision for the future.

The burning question for the STRUCTURAL Attribute is "HOW?" It realizes process prevents expensive problems.

The burning question for the SOCIAL Attribute is "WHO?" It realizes all business is relational.

E

A

Leaders in the first third of EXPRESSIVENESS may be seen as good listeners who will hear and consider all points of view.

Leaders in the third third of EXPRESSIVENESS may be seen as outgoing, energizing the company and inspiring others.

Leaders in the first third of ASSERTIVENESS may be seen as peacekeeping, promoting work and minimizing drama.

Leaders in the third third of ASSERTIVENESS may be seen as determined, keeping a foot on the gas and eyes on the road.

Leaders in the first third of FLEXIBILITY may be seen as focused, purposeful and having firm convictions.

Leaders in the third third of FLEXIBILITY may be seen as easygoing, welcoming change and encouraging others to keep options open.

Important Note: None of these attributes stand alone, but rather thread together in a way that produces WEteam magic.

What Are Your Strengths as a Leader?

As a reality check, ask your team what they consider to be your strengths.

F

The ANALYTICAL Attribute excels at being rational, thinking deeply, focusing on what needs to be done, relying on factual information, giving short directives and delegating certain details.

The CONCEPTUAL Attribute excels at being innovative and visionary, seeing the big picture, thinking globally, planning into the future and being open to out-of-the-blue inspirations.

The STRUCTURAL Attribute prefers tradition, clear rules and lines of authority, excels at handling details, brings order out of chaos, takes care of logistics and values efficiency.

The SOCIAL Attribute is interested in the well-being of others, and is encouraging, collaborative and empathic.

E

A

A leader in the first third of EXPRESSIVENESS is calm, quiet and poised, maintaining an even expression and allowing others to speak.

A leader in the third third of EXPRESSIVENESS is outgoing, walking the halls, always participating in a conversation and sharing information.

A leader in the first third of ASSERTIVENESS is peacekeeping, approachable, phrasing opinions carefully and going with the flow of the group.

A leader in the third third of ASSERTIVENESS is determined, competetive and decisive.

A leader in the first third of FLEXIBILITY is focused and purposeful, has firm convictions and insists on doing things their way.

A leader in the third third of FLEXIBILITY is fluid, doesn't mind change and is open to suggestions and ideas.

Important Note: None of these attributes stand alone, but rather thread together in a way that produces WEtcam magic.

Questions To Ask About Your Company

What to consider about your company.

F

ANALYTICAL thinkers might ask: Are the stakeholders happy? Could the company's systems be improved or updated? Are the current employees achieving maximum productivity?

CONCEPTUAL thinkers might ask: Is the company bringing out new products? Does Research and Development have enough resources? Are the current employees effectively connected to the company's vision?

STRUCTURAL thinkers might ask: Are there correct processes in place to deliver the company's goods or services? Are these processes efficient? Are the employees' roles well defined?

SOCIAL thinkers might ask: Are our client relationships in good standing? Are any changes coming that will adversely affect anyone? Are the current employees engaged?

E

A

Those in the first third of EXPRESSIVENESS may want to know if the environment is calm and quiet.

Those in the third third of EXPRESSIVENESS may want to know if the environment is animated and outspoken.

Those in the first third of ASSERTIVENESS may want to know if the company is performing steadily.

Those in the third third of ASSERTIVENESS may want to know if the company is performing at high risk.

Those in the first third of FLEXIBILITY may want to know if the company is laser-focused.

Those in the third third of FLEXIBILITY may want to know if the company is comfortable with change, revisions and/or interruptions.

Important Note: None of these attributes stand alone, but rather thread together in a way that produces WEteam magic.

Principle #2

EMBRACE THE *SCRATCHY*

Uncomfortable Is the New Norm

In Principle #1: Leadership Is an Inside Job, you became comfortable by getting to know yourself. In this principle, I'd like you get very uncomfortable by embracing the scratchy. What do I mean by that? When something takes you out of your comfort zone, I call that feeling being *scratchy*. Sometimes we're thrown out of our comfort zone by outside forces, but this chapter is about purposeful, self-motivated change for you and your greatest asset: your employees.

Why should you care about getting scratchy? Because scratchiness is the opposite of putting your head in the sand and trying to hang on to the status quo. Feeling uncomfortable is linked to sound business practices like continuous innovation, being frank about any problems that exist, and always scanning the horizon for future challenges so your business can respond quickly and nimbly. Getting out of your comfort zone may require restating company goals, pruning processes or people, confronting difficult topics, and being honest about longstanding problems for the first time. It also shows up in positive ways such as being open-minded about what your employees tell you, restating company goals, having permission to take risks and fail up, being able to admit a mistake without fear, welcoming creativity, and building your skills in personal preferences that you do not have.

The idea of reaching a state of comfortable stasis is a dangerous myth. The human body, for example, is in a constant state of flux, building up and tearing down, up-regulating, down-regulating, and recalibrating through feedback loops. If a human body is not growing and changing, it is dying. Like a human body, a business in stasis is dead. According to Andy Krupski, CEO of The Hive Strategic Marketing in Canada, "There is a school of thought that if an enterprise is not dedicating 10% of its annual topline growth to developing strategies that will disrupt its own business model, then failure is assured."

There are innumerable examples of companies that failed to embrace the scratchy, including businesses we thought were unsinkable such as the *Titanic*:

- Blockbuster Video had years to adapt to changing technology but never did. Although they knew their late fees were annoying their customers, they made so much money off them that they could not get scratchy enough to think of a different business model. One disgruntled customer was so irritated by $40 in late fees for renting *Apollo 13* that he started a competing company: Netflix.
- At one time, Eastman Kodak seemed invulnerable, but it failed to stay scratchy and open to change. An engineer at Kodak actually invented the first digital camera, but the company *kept it a secret* because the new camera did not use Kodak film.
- The venerable Sears, Roebuck and Company, founded in 1886, started out as a giant mail-order catalog – like an old-fashioned version of Amazon.com. Maybe they should have stayed that way. Today, Amazon has lapped Sears several times, and while other retailers were trying new products and services, Sears just stayed… Sears. Now the company has closed so many stores and sold off so many of its iconic brands that it has lost its own brand. The current head of Sears was named "the most hated CEO in America" in 2016, perhaps because he never leaves his comfort zone – his home in Florida – and manages only by video conferencing.
- Westinghouse Electric, also founded in 1886, was a household name for decades, holding many thousands of patents and manufacturing everything from electrical parts to home appliances. The company built the first nuclear reactor and then later made the gigantic commitment to build four nuclear reactors in Georgia and South Carolina. All four projects missed deadlines by years and ran wildly over budget – plus inspectors discovered builders had made serious construction errors that had to be fixed. Sometimes getting scratchy means facing issues you would rather ignore. Westinghouse over-promised on their timelines and budgets, failed to correct the problems, and went bankrupt.

Going outside your comfort zone helps you create more meaningful connections to your work, encourages personal growth, etches new neurological pathways in your brain, and makes you a better leader. Embracing the scratchy also allows better understanding of your employees and ensures they feel valued, engaged, and challenged.

WHAT EXACTLY IS *THE SCRATCHY*?

- If you're completely comfortable with your job every day, you're doing it wrong. It's not possible to learn, move ahead, or acquire new skills without 1) adding yet another task to your to-do list, and 2) getting outside your comfort zone and feeling scratchy. Naturally we tend to ignore the challenges or opportunities that make us uncomfortable. However, these often are the things we should be doing first – either to catch up to where the business needs to be, or in the interest of getting ahead of the curve and being ready to shape the future.
- This is not going to be the 50 millionth book on how to usher your company through corporate changes. It's not about being stuck in a merger, preparing your employees for a new system, or dealing with other company issues that are forced upon you. This principle is about getting yourself out of your comfort zone and making some changes that will be very good for you, very good for your people, and very good for your business.

SCRATCHINESS FOR YOU

As a leader, you can set a great example for your employees by being willing to take risks, try new things, and admit when you're out of your comfort zone.

First you must know yourself. As you read in Principle #1, self-awareness is the key to being an effective leader. Know how you think and behave. Recognize your values. Acknowledge both your talents and least-used attributes. Observe how you respond to a variety of leadership challenges, such as trying to influence others or giving a keynote address. Reflect upon your own leadership style. Be brutally honest with yourself. How could you change for the better?

- Be authentic. People immediately sense when you're faking your way through something, which erodes their trust and confidence in you.
- Acknowledge any areas that already make you feel scratchy.
- Challenge yourself to do at least one thing that feels scratchy every week.
- Try working through your least favorite Emergenetics Attributes to make them stronger.
- Take risks. Be fearless. Don't worry about the possibility of failing or looking foolish. You are human and everyone knows that already.
- Be open-minded. Reconsider previous decisions. Evaluate non-negotiables that actually are negotiable.
- Ask for feedback about how you are doing. Ask open-ended questions to get thoughtful answers. Don't ask unless you're willing to address the answers.

Your employees do not have the same preferences you do. For example, perhaps you're most comfortable picking up the phone and making a quick call. This seems perfectly natural to you, but some people hate the telephone. A call from you will scare them to death and make them very uncomfortable. (Note to those individuals: Try using the phone once in a while!) Communicate with your people in a variety of formats, some of which may make *you* feel scratchy, including phone calls, emails, face-to-face conversations, meetings, handwritten notes, and surveys.

SCRATCHINESS FOR YOUR EMPLOYEES

Your goal is a welcoming, supportive corporate environment that harmoniously accommodates people with different Profiles. Everybody will have to get a little scratchy to accommodate each other's attributes, but the results are well worth it. You will not end up with a workforce out of *The Stepford Wives* – you'll have a diverse group of people who know how to cooperate.

- Team members can begin by honoring each other's Profiles, and making the effort to flex their attributes in order to better appreciate each other and communicate more effectively.
- When employees already know each other's preferences, their action groups can get more done, more quickly (see Principle #4: Creating a Meeting of the Minds).
- Greater understanding of each other creates an atmosphere in which employees feel valued and challenged. This corporate culture increases employee engagement and job satisfaction.

SCRATCHINESS FOR YOUR BUSINESS

Allow your employees to embrace the scratchy. You can encourage them to get out of their comfort zones by modeling scratchiness and by cultivating a corporate culture that is not punitive. Know how your team members think and behave, their learning styles, their preferred ways of working, and what situations or people will make them feel scratchy.

- An adaptable work force already is shaping the future, while a fearful or disengaged work force resists change.
- A transparent environment – one in which people share how they think and behave – encourages greater engagement because there is a minimum of hidden agendas, head games, office politics, and negativity.
- Greater engagement means better employee retention, which in turn means keeping and promoting your people as they become more skilled instead of losing them to other companies.
- Encourage your employees to stretch their skills and take calculated risks. Show support when you know they are working out of their least preferred attributes. When they know you trust them, they will be more willing to push themselves when they are feeling scratchy.

- A corporate climate without fear promotes honesty, innovation, creativity, engagement, and learning. Give your workers permission to find meaning in failure and push through feeling scratchy to success.

HOW WE EMBRACE THE *SCRATCHY* IN OUR OFFICE

We embrace the scratchy every day. New employees regularly comment about the differences between our Emergenetics culture and their experiences within more traditional corporate climates. We do things differently around here. Everything is deliberately coordinated to produce a productive and healthy corporate environment. Everything we do is intentional, from the way we use our Profiles to understand each other, to the way we run our meetings, to our office decor, to the floor plan, and even the lightbulbs we use.

Following is a story that shows what is normal for our office. You might consider Emergineering some of these ideas into your company culture, even if they seem scratchy to you now.

NIKKI'S STORY

I hurried into the office one day after being out of town, and a new employee was sitting at a desk by the front door.

"Who are you?" I inquired.

"My name is Nikki," she asserted, briefly removing her hands from the keyboard. "Who are you?"

Snarkily I replied, "I am Geil, the person who signs your paycheck."

"That's nice," Nikki said, returning to her keyboard.

I ran into my office, grabbed what I needed for my next trip, and left feeling annoyed with myself that I had given her a testy answer. After all, I knew better. Research shows that an employee will be happier at her job if her leader has a conversation with her in the beginning.

> Two days later I returned and went back to Nikki's desk. I apologized, and said, "Let's talk for a few minutes so we can get to know each other better."
>
>   "Oh, I don't care about all that fluffy stuff," she answered, briefly looking up from her computer. "I am just going to get my job done!" She lowered her eyes and returned to her keyboard.

My gut flipped as I retreated into the confines of my office, thinking grumpily that everyone is right about "those millennials." I am a gregarious driver (**Expressiveness/Assertiveness**), so I actually thought we were going to have a chat. But then I checked Nikki's Emergenetics reports, which indicated her competencies, preferences, and motivations. When I saw her Profile, everything made sense. Talking just for the sake of talking was not a priority for Nikki, which ordinarily would worry me about someone whose job included customer care. *However,* I reasoned, *if Nikki stays in this office long enough, we will teach her that it is all right to be data-driven, practical,* and *relational. She can learn to flex her **Social** preference, and she will still get her work done.*

NIKKI'S PROFILE

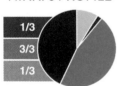

Here is Nikki's Emergenetics Profile. Note that her pie chart has preferences for both **Analytical** and **Structural** thinking. She has some Conceptual thinking but just a tiny sliver of **Social** thinking. She is reserved (first third of **Expressiveness**), determined (third third of **Assertiveness**), and absolute (first third of Flexibility). Her response to me was completely in character for someone without a **Social** preference who is at the quiet end of **Expressiveness**, the driving end of Assertiveness and the focused end of Flexibility. She really did just want to get her work done! Once again, it was not personal – it was Profile.

   In some corporate cultures, Nikki would have been gone in a minute after speaking to the CEO that way, but because she had landed a job at Emergenetics, I had access to her Profile and knew that incorporating Nikki into the team would be worth the effort. She would learn that she would have to tap into her **Social** attribute because she often has to speak with our Associates. Today, I frequently receive complimentary emails about her detailed work, as well as her thoughtful customer relations.

Nikki's previous job had been in a company with a generic working environment that had become quite negative. She was glad to be away from there, but she wasn't entirely prepared for how different she found our offices and our corporate culture. She was feeling scratchy starting her new job, and now I realize that her having a conversation with her new CEO right off the bat was disconcerting to her. When speaking to someone in authority, she prefers to be prepared and to have an agenda.

In our Emergenetics offices, we maintain a family-like, caring atmosphere. We accommodate the Profiles of a very diverse group of workers in as many ways as we can. We follow Tony Alessandra's platinum rule: Treat others the way they want to be treated! When we hire new employees, we check their Profiles, figure out their learning styles, and attempt to accommodate them so they complete their work brilliantly.

Everyone is free to talk to everyone else. We emphasize the positive and find different words to replace the negative (see Principle #3: The Language of Grace). We take every attribute into account when we make decisions. We don't have a lot of rules and regulations. If you get to work late, or need to help your son buy a corsage for the prom, or must take care of a sick child, the expectation is that you will get your work done soon as you are able.

We care about the health of our employees and believe that life is more than the time between vacations (see Principle #6: Let Your People Live to Work, Not Work to Live). The first time we told Nikki to take a "smoking break," she thought we had lost our minds. But because sitting is the new smoking, we encourage everybody to stop, get up, leave their work, and even walk around a bit outside.

Our walls are painted **Purple**, **Blue**, **Green**, **Red**, and Yellow, which fits our brand. Our walls also were outside Nikki's comfort zone at first, but she got used to them quickly. One day she was giving a client a quick tour of our offices and I overheard her saying, "Oh, the walls! When I came here, I thought there was a lot of color – plus each wall is different! There isn't a single room painted all the same. But the colors are part of our branding and our corporate culture. My office is blue and purple. It seemed strange, but I like it now."

MEET MARVIN, YOUR FUTURE EMPLOYEE

Emergenetics has been very successful in schools through our STEP (Student/Teacher Emergenetics Program). It is a separate division of Emergenetics that specializes in bringing our program into schools, working with educators who teach students from ages 10 to 18 using the *Emergenetics Youth Report*. The STEP program is how we met high school student Marvin.

The assistant principal of Marvin's school was telling us that she'd had to discipline him the day before. She had written him up for after-school detention, called his parents, and added a note in his permanent record saying that he had disrupted the entire school and was disciplined accordingly. Being an orderly person (Structural thinking) who was concerned about the school community at large (Social thinking), as well as being communicative (Expressiveness), no-nonsense (Assertiveness), and decisive (Flexibility), the assistant principal still was thinking the next day about Marvin's case, and wondering if there was anything else she should have done to ensure he would not wander into misbehaving again.

"Well, what did he do?" I asked.

It turns out Marvin had invented – all by himself – a smartphone application that could turn off all the electronics in his classroom. His teacher was trying to start a DVD when Marvin clicked on his app and made the TV monitor and all the computers in the room suddenly blink off.

Marvin was ecstatic. He leapt up from his chair and immediately headed for the hall, where he walked past classroom after classroom clicking his app, shutting down electronics and causing chaos. The most important thing to him was that his app *worked*.

I could not help chuckling.

"Do you think I should have done something else?" the assistant principal asked.

"Yes!" I replied. "You talked to him from your Structural/**Social** brain, but he heard what you said from his **Analytical**/Conceptual brain. Cheer him on for his intelligence, and move his energy to where it can be useful."

MARVIN'S PROFILE

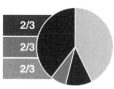

The assistant principal made Marvin a member of the school's Technology Club and also introduced him to the school's most proficient IT teacher. Marvin did not get out of detention, but he did find

MARVIN'S ASSISTANT PRINCIPAL

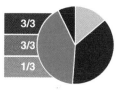

his tribe of fellow techies at the school and learned how to use his special powers constructively. Marvin was a senior, and his mother congratulated the assistant principal. It was the best year Marvin had ever had.

This child is your next employee. How will you be able to challenge him?

MEET EVERYONE'S NEEDS, NOT JUST YOUR OWN

As a leader, you must know yourself from the inside out. This will make you aware of any fears or biases you have that may prevent you from creating an optimal climate for all the different types of workers who make your company's success possible. Businesses today have many different kinds of corporate cultures, and you may be losing high performance employees to companies with more modern and accommodating environments.

What percentage of your employees are enthusiastic and fully engaged with their work? What is the mood in the morning? Does it take two cups of coffee before people start accomplishing anything? Stop for a moment and think about your employees – each one of them – and whether you are allowing them to work in the way they would like. Are you meeting the needs of different Profiles? How could you make your people happier and more productive?

- Even if it makes you feel self-conscious, post your Emergenetics Profile outside your door. You have nothing to hide. Be a proud representative of your attributes.
- Resolve to adapt at least one of the ideas in this chapter that takes you outside your comfort zone. Leap first. It will be OK.
- Do you keep doing things the same old way they've always been done without thinking why? I know people who still balance their checkbooks, even though millennials go through life without checks or even cash. Do your offices look like an episode of *The Twilight Zone*?
- Do you have personal biases that are affecting your corporate environment? How do *you* like to work? Are your preferences fair to everyone else? For example, look at your default method of communication – the one that suits your Profile most comfortably. Do you stretch your attributes to use more than this one approach? How accessible are you – really?
- Do executives and managers in your company demonstrate an acceptance for a wide variety of workplace behaviors and preferences? Is this acceptance modeled and lived at every level?
- Are you getting less out of your employees because they must all fall in line with a prescribed way of showing up to work? What about parents who have children to get to daycare or school? What about employees who prefer to come in late but will stay late as well?
- Is there a company-wide mandate about employees decorating their offices? What if they prefer to work with headphones, or like to put dragons on top of their computer monitors, or want to put their children's art up on the walls? Would letting employees work inside their comfort zone take you outside of yours?
- Are you holding back because the idea of changing your corporate environment makes *you* feel scratchy? Are there any company systems that should be updated but thinking about the inconvenience and expense makes you so uncomfortable that

you don't do anything? Are there any executives who should be fired but the process of showing them the door is just too difficult for you? Have you gotten complacent about the need to do the things that make you scratchy?

- Is there new technology that makes you uncomfortable? Can you navigate your smart TV and sound systems at home or do you have to call your kids? Technology isn't going to go backward.

Be bold. Be scratchy. Start somewhere. But while you're implementing a change, remember to think about all the attributes, not just your own.

AVOID A UNIFORM CORPORATE ENVIRONMENT

Recognizing that the brain needs to occasionally refresh itself throughout the day, businesses are making an effort to accommodate both work and leisure, sometimes in the same space. They may have spaces with tables for collaborating, as well as quiet areas for concentrating. This is better for the variety of people who work for you.

Some people work well in a uniform environment, but some don't.

A BRIEF HISTORY OF OFFICE SPACES

The word *corporate* has become synonymous with "gray, boring, and unimaginative." When you change your environment thoughtfully and with intention, your company's corporate climate and productivity will change as well.

With any office, there's always a conflict between the need for privacy and the need for openness, conversation, and collaboration. Which is more effective, interaction or autonomy? The answer depends upon the task as well as upon individual attributes. Workers need different options.

In the 1900s, the invention of the steel girder allowed builders to create huge rooms that could be filled up with banks of desks. Bosses looked on from private offices. These open rooms could fit a large number of employees, but they were noisy and stressful.

To encourage collaboration, designers tried pushing work-stations together, and setting them up like cells or pinwheels, but employees still were distracted, irritated, and exhausted. This did nothing to improve productivity, probably because every time we are interrupted, it takes 25 minutes for us to remember everything we were doing beforehand.

The first office cubicle was designed in 1968. The original cubicles had semiprivate spaces with low walls that allowed natural light to spread across the room. They had no doors, a giant surface for spreading out work, efficient files, and even standing desks. This design did not catch on until it was modified into a smaller, cheaper workstation – without the standing desk. By the 1990s, employers figured out they could cram more uniform cubicles together by using inexpensive modular walls. Midlevel employees got their own so-called private cubicles in which they could hear everyone else's conversations, smell each other's lunches, and catch each other's colds. Imagine having your cubicle right next to a high-traffic area like the water fountain, the coffee machine, or the bathrooms! Studies showed that being subjected to endless background noise disrupted concentration, impaired memory, and aggravated stress-related illnesses like migraines and ulcers. Next, forward-thinking employers went to the opposite end of the spectrum by "game-ifying" their environments. Some went *wild*. Some offices have couches, beanbag chairs, pool tables, snacks, random puzzles and brain teasers scattered about, and even slides between floors. Open, stimulating floor plans work best for energetic, outgoing employees – although even they may be too distracted by all the shiny things to concentrate. If this is your workplace, you probably won't hear anything from the quiet employees, who work best in a peaceful environment. If you go look, you might find one working behind a plant with headphones on.

Emergineering includes, but is not limited to, your floor plan. Creating new spaces that both satisfy and challenge your employees will move your company forward.

ONE COMPANY, MANY PROFILES

In our Emergenetics headquarters, some areas are quiet and some aren't. Some offices have doors and some don't. We accommodate both our headquarters and the separate STEP program on one floor. And, of course, our employees represent every kind of attribute, which is a challenge for every well-balanced organization.

MEGHAN'S
PROFILE

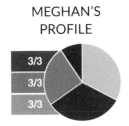

The main office, where you first enter the building, is very open, and the staff working there prefer it that way. They are all calm by nature (**Expressiveness**), and they are content working in silence. When others enter the front door, they are stunned by the quiet. This is where Nikki was working when I first met her, and she fit right in. Just one employee in this area, Meghan, is gregarious (**Expressiveness**), but she has learned to keep her vivacious energy under control while she works. This was a scratchy challenge for her, but her desire to work successfully with us is the motivation she needs to modulate her behavior while being surrounded by people who do not speak unless called upon to do so. Meghan still has a lot of energy around her innate need to converse, but fortunately she is adaptable (Flexibility) and has learned to channel that energy into all the talking she has to do on the phone in connection with her work.

GEIL'S
PROFILE

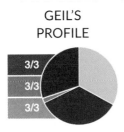

My son Morgan, Emergenetics President, and I both work near the main office. Our behaviors are identical. We each have a separate office with a door be-

MORGAN'S
PROFILE

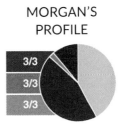

cause we're both animated (**Expressiveness**) and most of the time we're talking on the phone, in a meeting, or with employees. Both of us are far too loud for the group in the main office. We also get into heated discussions with each other, and because we're both debaters (**Assertiveness**), we never mind a good argument: it usually leads to another great idea. On the other hand, our spirited discussions are distressing to the nearby staff because we sound angry, and we ruin their peacefulness. The office manager actually asked us to *leave the offices* when we get annoyed with each other because we haven't been successful in learning how to disagree quietly and our debates upset the others.

The STEP crew is in another space down the hall, and they find ways to be gregarious but somehow still get their work done. Laughter comes from their office at any moment, and some of us visit them when we need a break.

The quiet room of the library is a sanctuary for soft-spoken people (**Expressiveness**) like those in our front office, but it's a jail for those who are irrepressible (**Expressiveness**). Changing from one office layout to another won't help your company's productivity unless you pay attention to the different attributes of your employees. You can see how we use different spaces to accommodate different attributes, and how the people who don't entirely fit in to a particular space make an effort to flex their attributes so they're part of their crowd.

SHARON'S
PROFILE

2/3
2/3
1/3

Sharon, our Director of Associate Development, has a corner office (formerly a closet) that suits her fine. She's interested in cerebral subjects (**Analytical**/Conceptual thinking) and is not passionate about what most other people are doing (**Social** thinking). She's glad there's no random foot traffic going by her office. If someone wants to see her, they know where to find her.

Sharon regularly goes to brainstorm with the STEP crew, who are naturally outgoing. Sharon explains, "I visit the STEP office with purposeful intent, but now I understand the need to indulge this group by giving them time to share stories about their weekend news involving children, dogs, and other miscellaneous events."

Having studied Emergenetics for many years, Sharon knows that people with her combination of **Analytical**/Conceptual thinking attributes generally believe they are smarter than everyone else. She adds, laughing, "Hear the arrogance in my voice? I don't deeply care about the STEP employees' brilliant children or grand-children, or someone's new puppy, or an uncle's visit to the hospital, but I know it will help everyone get along if I take an interest." Similarly, although Sharon enjoys the company of her coworkers at Emergenetics, she would not refer to them as "friends." For Sharon, and for most other **Analytical**/Conceptual thinkers, only a few relationships are deeply felt.

Sharon applies the platinum rule, stretches her natural preferences, and treats this group as they want to be treated. She just wants to get her work done, but she knows she needs to give the STEP crew time to release their outgoing energy first.

Sharon's combination of **Analytical**/Conceptual thinking is seen twice as often in men as in women (17% of men vs. 8.5% of women). In the corporate world, men with this profile typically do not prefer to be seen as heartfelt and sympathetic. Left to themselves, they're more interested in thinking about data, big-picture systems, and solutions. The way they show their passion is by accomplishing amazing projects. When you ask them about their work, they will speak about what they believe is necessary for the team. They're not interested in pleasing the team's human element. Instead, their work is a gift to the team because it will make it easier for team members to move forward with what they must accomplish.

Managers with **Analytical**/Conceptual thinking preferences and no **Social** preference can be intimidating, particularly if they are at the quiet end of the **Expressiveness** spectrum. They seldom see any reason to leave their intellectual tower and most likely abhor idle chitchat. If a male manager with this Profile skips the office party, people may notice his absence with relief and have another adult beverage. On the other hand, because Sharon is female, people are surprised that she doesn't go to office parties, and that she doesn't especially care about the personal lives of others – something about which Sharon is not apologetic. Not all women are wired with a **Social** preference.

You might be surprised to learn that in addition to her Emergenetics work, Sharon is a spiritual adviser. She says she does not need to care about people's puppies to recognize what is going on in their lives. In fact, she thinks a little distance makes her better at seeing her clients' issues. However, Sharon will modulate her attributes to meet other people where they are to make them feel comfortable. This is scratchy for her, but then others are able to see themselves in her, which helps her work successfully with them.

Sharon has become extremely adept at flexing her attributes. This is an essential skill in counseling, as well as any time you have many people working together. I'll be returning to this subject often. Scratchiness is good because skills can't be developed unless people are given the opportunity to practice. Many employees develop improved self-confidence when they get out of their usual comfort zone and realize they're able to collaborate with almost anyone.

Even when you hire for fit, there still will be scratchiness in the company – and that is not a negative thing. Feeling scratchy can be a great incentive to move forward and grow. Emergineering will help you recast any pain points as opportunities to stretch and to set new goals.

HOW WE EMERGINEERED OUR MEETINGS

Our offices are designed for learning, and we stay on top of the latest neurological research to benefit ourselves and our clients. This section will share with you our best meeting practices – those that allow us to run the company efficiently and to honor every attribute. Attendance at these meetings is mandatory, and they are held during work hours. Some are giddier than others, but they are not office parties. Some types of meetings are scheduled weekly, whereas others only take place once a year, but all contribute profoundly to how we meet our personal and business goals.

Without regular meetings like this, it's easy to get caught up in everyday challenges, and before you know it something is going off the rails. Everyday busyness can be so distracting that we lose track of our priorities – those things that are the most valuable for us and for the company.

STRUCTURAL (GREEN) MEETINGS

We hold Green meetings every Wednesday. These are designed to let the left hand know what the right hand is doing.

- We start and end on time. By starting with a centering exercise (discussed later in the chapter) we make sure no one is late, ever.
- We follow an agenda.
- Every report has an objective.
- All information is narrowed to fit into 30 minutes.

These characteristics are satisfying to the employees with a lot of Structural neurological connections in their brains. They are frustrated by free-form meetings that to them seem to go on forever.

SOCIAL (RED) MEETINGS

Red meetings are all about teambuilding. Each department picks a month to plan.

- In January, we celebrate the Chinese New Year, and red envelopes are given to each employee. This helps us remember that we are a global company. At the same time, our Singapore office does something similar.
- In February, we celebrate Valentine's Day. This year, the theme was Fond of You Fondue Party
- In April, we always go for Barbecue and Bowling to celebrate our knockout year.

One of the world's largest breweries originally gave us the idea for **Red** meetings. At one of their **Red** parties that we were invited to, one of our employees who is known for her sociable nature (**Expressiveness**) approached a man who was sitting at the end of the bar, speaking to no one. She asked him why he was sitting there by himself at a **Red** meeting filled with people who had a preference for

Social thinking. He said, "I want to find out what **Social** people do at a **Red** meeting." He had no preference for **Social** thinking, and his behaviors indicated he preferred to be alone. He said, "I have no need to be at this party. I simply came to analyze the situation and learn what happens at a **Red** meeting." He will probably never attend another.

MARTHA'S
PROFILE

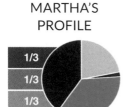

1/3
1/3
1/3

One of our employees, Martha, has data-driven (**Analytical**) and methodical (**Structural**) thinking preferences. She seldom speaks (**Expressiveness**), never makes a scene (**Assertiveness**), and is focused (**Flexibility**) in everything she does. Because I am in and out of the office so much, months may go by during which I never hear Martha's voice.

Martha is obligated to come to our **Red** meetings, but she is not obligated to enjoy them. She chooses not to participate in any revelry, and instead sits in a corner reading a book. She never told anyone that she doesn't enjoy bowling, but then again she didn't have to. It isn't an issue. The other employees all know her Profile and recognize that this is simply who Martha is.

CONCEPTUAL (YELLOW) MEETINGS

Yellow meetings are all about the big picture for the business. We have one Yellow meeting at the beginning of each year.

- We review the previous year's accomplishments.
- We congratulate ourselves for the amount of work we did.
- We set a long-term vision for where we want to be in the future.
- We set short-term goals for the following year.
- The last goal is always a *Happy Surprise.* It's important to have open-ended goals so you can invite positive energy into the business.

A recent *Happy Surprise* was the addition of our first Emergenetics representative in Africa. At the beginning of that year, it was not one of our goals. Through hard work and good fortune, we expanded our global footprint to new territories.

ANALYTICAL (BLUE) MEETINGS

We hold a **Blue** meeting every July. This meeting is based on analyzing data and financial information.

- We measure our progress toward our objectives for the year.
- We review the status of our finances.
- We determine how we will proceed for the second half of the year.

Just like a household budget, a company budget has ebbs and flows of income and expenses. Because one of our values is maintaining a sense of family, transparency is important to us. If revenues indicate we need to curb expenses, everyone plays a part in minimizing expenditures. Privately owned companies are often reluctant to share financial information with their employees, but this meeting is particularly applicable to them.

CENTERING

Imagine being asked to sit in a circle, being invited to close your eyes, then using your breath to scan your body for any tension, and finally being asked to pay attention to your breath again to release the tension. We begin every meeting with this centering exercise to get our brains focused. It is conducted in silence for two or three minutes, and then the timekeeper invites everybody to open their eyes and the meeting continues.

When we first started this practice, many members of the staff felt scratchy about it. They were willing to go along, but there was some reluctance that showed up as rustling and movement during the three minutes of quiet. What finally sold everyone on centering was the efficiency and focus with which we're able to conduct our meetings. We're able to cover a lot more information in 30 minutes than before. After doing this for several months, we have noticed an immediate depth of silence as everybody releases their day's frustrations instead of letting them carry over into the meeting. Now when we begin, everyone in the room becomes instantly silent – even the most recent employees, who may find this a bizarre way to start a meeting.

Remember Nikki, our new employee? She felt out of her element at her first team meeting when she was introduced to two of our office rituals: "centering" before the meeting, and "reflection" after it (more about reflection in a moment). These practices put Nikki at a loss, but now, after a couple of months, she enjoys the centering, and we know we will hear a meaningful reflection from her at the end of every meeting after she has had time to think about what she wants to say.

At this point, you may be wondering if you should continue reading, because you can't imagine selling this idea to your people and it sounds like cosmic woo-woo psychobabble. But research is on your side. Meditation, or centering, releases stress and lowers blood pressure. When people are relaxed and not distracted by worries, the brain releases oxytocin – known as the trust hormone because it reduces fear, enhances feelings of closeness, and promotes group cooperation. Oxytocin encourages people to trust their group leader and even helps explain why people who feel connected walk in tandem and clap in unison.

Our centering exercise has benefits that extend well beyond our meetings. Intentionally building social ties at work is linked to improved performance and engagement. Research spanning several years shows that, compared with people at low-trust companies, people at high-trust companies report 74% less stress, 106% more energy at work, 50% higher productivity, 13% fewer sick days, 76% more engagement, 29% more satisfaction with their lives, and 40% less burnout. How do you feel about centering now?

LEADING THE CENTERING EXERCISE

The last question you're probably wondering about is: Who will lead the centering at your meetings? It doesn't have to be you.

Someone from your team would probably be happy to volunteer because many people have now incorporated mindfulness into their lifestyles. Or you can hire a consultant. Do you remember Sharon, the spiritual adviser I mentioned earlier? We have her lead our three minutes of centering at the beginning of every meeting.

Some of your people will take to centering like ducks to water. We've noticed that individuals with a lot of imagination (Conceptual thinking) who are also open-minded (Flexibility) slide into the process immediately. Others may be more skeptical, and it may take them several weeks to be persuaded. The initial scratchiness of this practice may make you want to forget the whole thing, but please persevere. The top brains in the country are behind you.

REFLECTION

In general, we do not take enough time to reflect. We are so busy *doing* that we don't take time for *thinking*. This applies to every human being except babies, and who knows what they're doing. Some people are more likely than others to mull things over, but reflection benefits everyone.

We end every Emergenetics meeting by briefly sharing our personal reflections about what the group just discussed. Time is built into the agenda for this. We have found that:

- The process of personal reflection extracts additional meaning from each meeting and cements it in our minds.
- Hearing each other's thoughts gives us more ideas to consider, often leading to new, constructive avenues of thought.
- An added benefit to ruminating about the meeting and articulating our thoughts for each other is that this can be a profound exercise in vulnerability and team bonding.

Typically, the leader identifies a question for the group to reflect on at the end of the meeting. Generally, the question has some reference to the meeting and how it affects each person. Sample questions could be:

- What insights did I gain from this meeting?
- What did I learn about myself?
- Our profits are up. What does this mean to my department, and what can I learn from this?
- Our client is not happy. What have I learned from this experience?

As you can see, these the questions are related back to the individual. This helps everybody relate the information from the meeting to ways in which they can grow, which ultimately will benefit the growth of the organization.

People who are tranquil (**Expressiveness**) prefer to have some time to organize their thoughts, so it's a good idea to allow a moment before the first person speaks. Convergent (**Analytical/Structural**) thinkers likely will be skeptical of this process, but they'll give it a go if they trust you. Over time, their reflections often become the most meaningful. Our employee Brad, a quiet, convergent (**Analytical/Structural**) thinker, initially scoffed at the idea of taking valuable time for reflections. Most likely, you'll have at least one or two people like Brad on your staff. Although his initial reflections were perfunctory, over time the value of reflections became apparent to him. Now we all wait to hear Brad's thoughts, which invariably are deep and thought-provoking.

We begin by asking, "Who wants to go first?" and then go around the table in order. No one is allowed to interrupt or cross-talk until everyone has finished. No one may demur. After this, the leader asks for "reflections on the reflections." The follow-on reflections that surface usually are beneficial for the entire group. Eventually, with practice, all the reflections will become deeper.

Reflection taps into all aspects of your experiences, clarifies your thinking, and helps your mind consolidate what matters and what you wish to achieve. Anchoring and deepening your learning also adds neural circuitry to your brain and expands the cerebral cortex. Reviewing what works, making connections, setting goals, and building your brain – what's not to like about a little ruminating?

IMPLEMENTATION STEPS

1. Challenge yourself to do something that feels scratchy. Try centering in your next meeting.
2. Give your employees permission to risk and fail forward.
3. Take time for reflection.

TEMPLATES FOR PRINCIPLE #2:
EMBRACE THE SCRATCHY

1. WHAT MAKES EACH ATTRIBUTE FEEL *SCRATCHY*?
What takes you out of your comfort zone?

2. HOW TO EMBRACE THE *SCRATCHY*
You can learn to like new things.

3. HOW DIFFERENT PREFERENCES ACCEPT CHANGE
If a change is definitely ahead, don't try to fight it. Save your energy and process it through your thinking and behavioral preferences.

What Makes Each Attribute Feel "Scratchy"?

What takes you out of your comfort zone?

F

ANALYTICAL thinkers will likely be uncomfortable moving forward without knowing the objectives of the goal and the data supporting it.

CONCEPTUAL thinkers will likely need to feel connected to the big picture. They may be uncomfortable feeling constrained by limits set on the goal.

STRUCTURAL thinkers will likely need set plans and guidelines. They may be uncomfortable without set processes to achieve the goal.

SOCIAL thinkers will likely need to see how the goal will affect others. They may feel uncomfortable if they don't have a chance to connect with other people to discuss the goal.

E

A

Those in the first third of EXPRESSIVENESS may be uncomfortable if they are put on the spot in a group.

Those in the third third of EXPRESSIVENESS may be uncomfortable if they don't have a chance to voice their thoughts.

Those in the first third of ASSERTIVENESS may be uncomfortable in situations involving conflict.

Those in the third third of ASSERTIVENESS may be uncomfortable if they have to work at a restricted pace.

Those in the first third of FLEXIBILITY may be uncomfortable if they have to change course at the last minute.

Those in the third third of FLEXIBILITY may be uncomfortable if they are not able to explore alternatives.

Important Note: None of these attributes stand alone, but rather thread together in a way that produces WEteam magic.

How To Embrace the "Scratchy"

You can learn to like new things.

F

The ANALYTICAL brain may think about how this change has been beneficial, rather than focusing on the data. Access the SOCIAL brain to think about the human element. Try to accept the change without having supporting data.

The CONCEPTUAL brain may think about the details and logistics involved in this change. Go to the STRUCTURAL brain to figure out steps for implementing this change. Try to accept the change without thinking about the larger vision.

The STRUCTURAL brain may look at the long-term payoff of this change. Go to the CONCEPTUAL brain to see the big picture. Try to accept the change without thinking about the logistics.

The SOCIAL brain may think about people, instead of the difference this change may make in profits. With the ANALYTICAL brain, look at this change from a rational perspective. Try to accept the change without being emotional.

E

A

Challenge your first third EXPRESSIVENESS and speak up about any reservations you have.

Challenge your third third EXPRESSIVENESS by listening to others before you announce your thoughts.

Challenge your first third ASSERTIVENESS by standing up for an idea that has value.

Challenge your third third ASSERTIVENESS by being aware of pushing too hard, and stepping back to examine other points of view.

Challenge your first third FLEXIBILITY if this is a change you don't like and keep an open mind, trying not to shut down right away.

Challenge your third third FLEXIBILITY by thinking about why this particular course of action is the best choice.

Important Note: None of these attributes stand alone, but rather thread together in a way that produces WEteam magic.

How Different Attributes Accept Change

If a change is definitely ahead, don't try to fight it. Save your energy and process it through your Thinking and Behavioral Preferences.

F

ANALYTICAL thinkers may have logical reasons for being skeptical and may appear unemotional. They may need a sound reason for the change, research to justify it and time to ponder it.

CONCEPTUAL thinkers may be early adapters and energized by change in the beginning. They will likely connect with the ideology or big picture. They may summarize the change with a picture, word or motto.

STRUCTURAL thinkers may be cautious and feel stressed unless they are convinced the change is an improvement. They may need to know how it will affect the future. They may need specifics and background information and will likely prefer a plan with steps.

SOCIAL thinkers may have an emotional reaction and may take the change personally. They will likely be concerned about how it will affect others and may need to use stories and have conversations with others to process it.

E

A

Those in the first third of EXPRESSIVENESS may appear calm and approving, but they will likely need time alone to process the change internally.

Those in the third third of EXPRESSIVENESS may appear more accepting than they are. They will likely process their thoughts and emotions externally.

Those in the first third of ASSERTIVENESS may appear to be on board to ensure agreement with the team.

Those in the third third of ASSERTIVENESS may forget to ask the team if they are on board. They may address conflict swiftly and will likely want to speed things up.

Those in the first third of FLEXIBILITY may appear resistant. Once a new direction is defined they will likely be energized and stay the course.

Those in the third third of FLEXIBILITY may be prematurely seen as on board because of their willingness to discuss the change.

Important Note: None of these attributes stand alone, but rather thread together in a way that produces WEteam magic.

USING THE LANGUAGE OF GRACE

Words Are Powerful

The Language of Grace is not just words. It's an empowering and effective tool that creates behavioral changes. It starts with your making a conscious effort to choose different language patterns that emphasize positive thoughts and outcomes and then encouraging everyone else to do the same. As your workers become more fluent in this language, thinking patterns in the workplace begin to change. Eventually, these evolve into behavioral changes and an energized corporate climate.

THE QUIET ENGINEER

Kärcher is a family-owned company and the world's leading provider of efficient cleaning systems. Kärcher bases its reputation on top performance, innovation, and quality, so there is a constant drive to upgrade and improve its products.

A Kärcher engineer sent us an email saying his team had been struggling with a manufacturing issue they had not been able to solve. Their usual approach at Kärcher is to hold intense conversations and move on, but in this case their meetings had not been productive.

The team leader had been trained in Emergenetics, but as someone with a preference for **Analytical** thinking, he had been skeptical during the seminar and only had given it his perfunctory attention. In desperation, he decided to revisit what he had learned.

Realizing that he had made an oversight, the team leader reviewed the individual Profiles of his team, and discovered he had not heard from one engineer who was at the first third of **Expressiveness**. He quietly sought out this individual and asked him if he had any ideas for solving the problem.

The quiet engineer was not angry, or uncooperative, or withholding information. He just wasn't ready to speak in front of the entire team. Often, people in the first third of **Expressiveness** process information very deliberately, and they believe their ideas aren't welcome because the group has already moved on without them and identified the next step. In addition, this engineer was a junior member among many more vocal team members.

The team leader took a step outside Kärcher's typical corporate culture and sought out the quiet engineer's input. The team leader had written us to let us know that this person provided the suggestion that ultimately produced the solution the team needed. With the success of this experience, the team members today have shifted in the way they interact with each other.

As a leader, you deal every day not only with the skill sets of different employees, but also with their hearts, minds, self-esteem, and enthusiasm. At Emergenetics, we use the Language of Grace for two reasons:

1. To emphasize the positive, constructive, and optimistic. Thoughtless criticism or an offhand remark can leave employees reeling. Constructive words and carefully chosen phrases will help them feel supported and energized. Using the Language of Grace can mobilize and inspire your workers and create a positive workplace climate that reaches into every corner.

2. To honor each other's Profiles and deliberately use words and phrases that are most easily understood by your listeners. How people speak and what they hear are influenced by their preferences, and you can't assume that the meaning of whatever you say or write is inherently obvious. You could be speaking very clearly – to people just like you. Meanwhile people with other preferences are not getting the point as you intended. The Language of Grace will help create a corporate climate of improved communication.

ACCENTUATE THE POSITIVE – REALLY

Positive psychology is having a heyday right now, and there are numerous, well-researched, scientifically verifiable reasons why an optimistic outlook is good for your business. One study found that most optimistic leaders were rated at the 89th percentile of effectiveness, whereas their pessimistic counterparts were rated at only the 19th percentile. The same study concluded that the best workplace practices that leaders can use to increase morale include:

1. Treating mistakes as temporary setbacks
2. Concentrating on solutions rather than assigning blame
3. Celebrating positive news
4. Looking for value in unique perspectives
5. Focusing on long-term goals to keep team members engaged
6. Inspiring others with enthusiasm and even fun
7. Being humble enough to accept criticism and learn from it
8. Giving honest feedback in a helpful way.

I agree with this list, but I would begin it with an addition: Watching your words. They are an essential part of creating an energized and collaborative work force.

At Emergenetics, we constantly are striving to maintain our own positive culture while helping our clients do the same. When we can accentuate the positive and eliminate the negative, we do it wholeheartedly!

A large part of being a leader is motivating others. Keep in mind that positive messages are more effective than negative ones.

As you begin to think and speak positively, bear in mind that the brain cannot process a negative goal. If someone says, "Don't panic!" this immediately makes people panic. If someone says, "Stay calm, everyone," then the brain knows what to do. The slogan "Don't drink and drive" was never effective because the brain's takeaway message was "Drink and drive." This is why the slogan was changed to positive suggestions like, "Drive responsibly." In Europe you might hear, "Think how you drink," while in Asia one campaign is, "Have a good night out."

HOW NEGATIVE WORDS AFFECT THE BRAIN

Never doubt that words are powerful. When researchers put their subjects in an MRI machine and flashed the word *NO* at them for less than a second, their bodies immediately released dozens of stress-related neurotransmitters and hormones of the variety that disrupt normal brain function. These chemicals impair logic, reasoning skills, and language processing – that is, communication. All of this happens on a subconscious level in *under one second.*

When anxious people glance at a list of negative words (I won't spell them out!), they feel awful. If they take longer to read the list, they feel even worse. This can disrupt everything from their sleep to their ability to feel happiness. If they frown or say anything out loud ("Oh no!"), even more stress chemicals are released – and now the listener feels anxious, too. Words alone, even without any context, can magnify anxiety. They can make even the smallest exchange toxic, undermining trust and cooperation. Negative people are never alone in their misery because we are hard-wired to feel miserable along with them.

Words that provoke fear cause the release of destructive neurochemicals. Negative words that are spoken in anger ring alarm bells that can make people become irrational. The way to get off this train is to stop frowning and make a conscious effort to interrupt negative thinking; take time throughout the day to feel gratitude; think about words like *love, joy, peace,* and *compassion*; share happy events with others ... and use the Language of Grace. Positive words turn on specific genes that lower physical and emotional stress, and prompt the motivational centers of the brain into action. Language is a powerful part of determining corporate climate because choosing the right words makes everyone feel better, and also helps employees build more trusting relationships with each other.

USING POSITIVE WORDS THAT ENHANCE ENERGY

There is always more than one way to say something. Choose the way that projects more optimism and enthusiasm. Here are Dennison and Dennison's list of words that reduce or promote energy:

REDUCES ENERGY	ENHANCES ENERGY
Try	Do my best
I can't remember	I haven't remembered yet
I lost	I didn't win this time
I stopped	I haven't finished yet
I quit	I'm taking a break
This is a problem	This is a challenge
I hate	I'd prefer something else
I'm sorry I messed up	I'm sorry – how can I help fix this?
You never	Why don't we
If	When

VOCABULARY SWITCHES TO MAKE NOW

The Language of Grace emphasizes positivity, caring, and connectedness. Words convey respect (or disrespect), understanding (or lack of it), and approval (or disdain). As you saw above, small changes in vocabulary signal a big difference between a corporate climate that is indifferent and one that is encouraging, optimistic, and reassuring. A nonjudgmental corporate culture allows employees to fail forward and to be honest without fear of reprisal.

USE THE CORPORATE "WE"

You've undoubtedly heard of the royal "we," and the editorial "we." In our offices, we have the Emergenetics "WE," which stands for *Whole Emergenetics*. For us, "we" is an extra powerful word. For example, WEteams are extremely important because they include representation from every attribute. In our meetings, in our emails, and in our conversations with clients, we use WE as a collective term. This emphasizes the point that we do things together as a team – a WEteam. These are so crucial they have their own chapter: Principle #4: Using the Power of WE.

Using "we" not only closes the divide between "me" and "you" but also helps to bridge the divide between management and non-management, between women and men, and between those who have a preference for a certain attribute and those who do not. Our office includes a great diversity of Profiles, but "we" brings us all together. Once we begin to form divides in our language, we form divides in real life.

Posted on one of our walls in the Singapore office is the line, "We help each other be at our best." This is a reminder that one of us is never better than the rest of us. It's also a reminder to reach out to colleagues when we see something not working or notice people not functioning at their best. Helping can range from sending friendly reminders (if we know someone tends to forget) to being a buddy so a job becomes less scary. Competition in the office, if any, always is in the spirit of nudging others to be at their best and helping them progress. And when we see someone else contribute at their best, we celebrate their wins, because their success becomes ours.

SAY "I'M DOING MY BEST!" INSTEAD OF "I'M TRYING!"

A word we remove is *try*. Coaches know this. They never say to the team, "Try hard." Better to say, "Go out, do your best, and have fun." Remind your people not to answer, "I'm *trying!*" when someone asks how they are progressing. This response has frustration and failure built in. Instead they can answer, "I'm doing my best!" This resonates with aspiration and determination. Start doing this in your office and notice the difference.

EXPLAIN WHAT YOU ARE DOING INSTEAD OF SAYING "I'M BUSY!"

There's another four-letter word that we've done our best to banish from our offices, and we've encouraged our clients to do the same. It's not a word we ever want to fall upon the tender ears of our Emergenetics family. That word is *BUSY*.

So how do we avoid using that four-letter word, and how does it help us? When it comes down to it, busy is a copout. By eliminating that escape hatch from our vocabulary, we encourage people to thoughtfully consider what they are doing rather than dismissing out of hand a well-intended interruption, or a request to meet or speak.

When you really are up to your ears and up against a deadline and feeling the stress, be honest but without saying "busy." A simple, "I'm sorry, I am actively working on several projects with pending deadlines. Let's aim for tomorrow." At the very least, the other person will appreciate what you are up against and may even offer to help.

When someone asks, "How is your day going?" the optimal answer is not "I'm busy!" Everybody is busy! A better answer is something like, "I am vigorously pursuing my goals." Our Associates in London say, "I am frantically plate spinning." Though that isn't exactly positive, it does make me laugh!

COMMUNICATION IS EVERYTHING

Effective communication is so much more than just talking. At Emergenetics, we are acutely aware that people with different Profiles will speak differently and interpret words differently. Two people with the best of intentions may talk at cross-purposes because their brains are just not wired the same way.

Communication has different moving parts that all are equally important, so if you really want to be understood, you must flex your own attributes to match those of your listener(s). With every exchange, think:

- How can I present my thoughts in a positive, energetic way?
- How can I make sure my words will be interpreted correctly by people with different Profiles?
- I must check to make sure they understood what I thought I was communicating.
- I must remember to take their Profiles into consideration as I focus on their feedback.

The same recommendations apply to writing and speaking, whether you're talking one-on-one, speaking to a crowd, writing emails, writing thank-you notes, or sending memos to staff. Incidentally, you'll always want to maintain your careful standards, even when you're talking about people in their absence. You never know what will be repeated – plus, your listeners will be wondering what you say behind their backs about them.

The *intent/impact gap* occurs when people try to explain something, but their words have entirely unintended and unanticipated consequences. Often, the resulting misunderstandings can lead to even worse problems because of the assumptions that follow, such as, "He has no idea what he is talking about!" or, "She cannot take even basic instructions!"

Let's say leaders with an abstract brain (**Analytical**/Conceptual) are giving an assignment to their teams. They're very focused on the target, and that's the only thing they discuss. They're not especially interested in the details, and they would be fine with having someone else explore the options available in completing the task.

If the people receiving the assignment also are abstract thinkers (**Analytical**/Conceptual), they may understand the challenge and be eager to take it on.

If the people receiving the assignment are concrete thinkers (Structural/**Social**), they may be lost. They will complain to colleagues that they've just been assigned a task without any of the information they need – no timeline, no budgetary considerations, no direction for additional support, etc. They will conclude that the leader might not even know how to complete the task – otherwise, the information they need would have been provided.

THE EMERGENETICS APP

To Emergineer your conversations, consider the way others want to be treated. But how do you know what that *is* until you know more about them?

Start by looking at their Profiles. People think I have special powers of discernment, but everything I know about others

I learned from simply studying people with different Profiles. Without having met someone, I can look at their Profile and, of course, anticipate how they think and how they will behave. I know not to overwhelm a quiet person with my love of conversation (**Expressiveness**), and not to try to impress someone who follows the rules (Structural thinking) with my best crazy stories. From the Profile, I usually can make educated guesses about what this person considers helpful, what motivates them, what they respect in other people, how they prefer to receive information, how they make decisions, how they feel about change, how they will perceive me, and so on. Looking at all of their personal preferences takes me out of myself so that I can concentrate on the individual. When I take the time to meet others where they are, I get more out of my conversation and also minimize the chances of miscommunications.

Everyone who has taken the online Profile has access to our free Emergenetics smartphone app. If you're part of a group, all of the Profiles in your group are automatically uploaded into the app so you can connect with one another and can get instant access to the Profiles of everyone you know who is associated with Emergenetics.

SHERYL'S
PROFILE

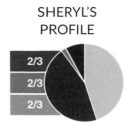

Sheryl is people-oriented (**Social**) and inventive (Conceptual thinking). She reports to Penny, the CFO of the corporation who is da-ta-driven (**Analytical**)

PENNY'S
PROFILE

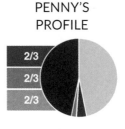

and also ingenious (Conceptual thinking), like Sheryl. Although Sheryl and Penny have worked together for some time, Sheryl still goes to the Emergenetics app every time she's about to meet with Penny for a refresher course in how to build rapport with her: what words to use, how to apply the platinum rule, and how to build mutual respect. The app allows Sheryl to base her conversation with Penny on her bona fide strengths rather than Sheryl's best guess about Penny's abilities. Each exchange they have strengthens their relationship, and each positive conversation is embedded in their workplace climate.

USING THE "THIRDS"

The Emergenetics Profile is a strengths-based assessment. When we describe a Profile, or any element of the Profile, we're very aware of using strengths-based language. When you receive your own Emergenetics Profile, we will tell you to value your uniqueness and work through your strengths.

We studiously avoid using judgmental language about the different attributes. For example, people who do not have a particular attribute are not missing anything. They're just fine the way they are. Similarly, although we refer to attributes that people do have as strengths, we do not refer to the attributes they do not have as weaknesses.

As you already have seen, each Behavioral Attribute is pictured on a spectrum that is divided into thirds. Rather than saying people are not very expressive (which sounds like a criticism), we say they are quiet (**Expressiveness**). To avoid saying people are impatient (also somewhat insulting), we say they are driving (Assertiveness). Instead of saying people are inflexible (another word with negative connotations), we say they are focused (Flexibility).

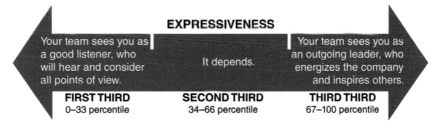

We describe the Behavioral Attributes in thirds because:

1. This presentation is reflective of the general population, and
2. It helps us steer stay away from value-laden words such as high or low, which have no meaning tied to the Profile.

In this book, we avoided using *first third*, *second third*, and *third third* as much as we could because this terminology feels awkward when you're not used to it. However, once you become serious about Emergineering your company, you will find that speaking in thirds liberates you from judging other people.

Everyone possesses some degree of **Expressiveness**, Assertiveness, and Flexibility, but also is able to flex their preferences according to the circumstances. People who are at the third third of **Expressiveness** will need some time to re-energize after being around people for an extended amount of time. People who are in the first third of **Assertiveness** may flex their preference to become more driving if their values are compromised. People who are third third in Flexibility may become steadfast over something that for them is a personal deal breaker. In general, however, everyone has an innate set point for each behavioral attribute that can be described in thirds.

ADDRESSING PEOPLE WITH DIFFERENT PROFILES

Part of the Language of Grace is honoring the differences among people by speaking to different individuals in a way that suits their Profiles. If I value my conversation with you, then I will speak in a way that resonates with you.

You will understand me better if I make an effort to use language as you do. Whether I'm getting to know you, collaborating with you, selling something to you, giving you an assignment, or mediating a disagreement that involves you, I will try to match the way you speak (as well as the way you behave). For examples, see the template at the back of this chapter, How to Speak to Different Attributes.

ANALYTICAL

People with a preference for **Analytical** thinking are usually rational and efficient. If they're interested in a subject, they'll gather the best available data and drill down for information (they're divers rather than skimmers). They prefer to examine every angle of a topic. In conversation, less is more. They prefer precise, logical words 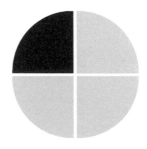 and summaries and do not want long discussions or emotional pleas. They're fast learners and are used to assimilating information quickly, so when speaking to people with this preference, do not bog them down with a lot of details. Cut to the bottom line and give them key facts, conclusions based on accurate data, and any material they need to examine. They do prefer to have an opportunity to ask questions. If they ask you a question and you do not know the answer, don't even try to bluff your way through; just tell them you'll get back to them later. *Do not* make a mistake because they'll never forget.

STRUCTURAL

People with a preference for Structural thinking are usually practical, methodical, and detail-oriented. They prefer clear, articulate words and conversations. They excel at absorbing a lot of facts and creating order out of chaos. However, do not give them information in a chaotic way. Present all the details they need in an orderly way, 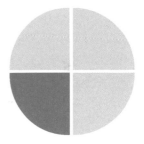 along with clear directions. They find written information helpful. Remember to stay on track – no tangents or surprises, and try not to spring anything unexpected on them. People with this preference have a strong sense of order, and they'll follow any guidelines, rules, or policies. If your discussion veers into any territory that is unfamiliar or has not already been established as a company priority, you may encounter a wall of resistance. They appreciate being notified about any time constraints and being given a chance to ask for clarification and additional information.

SOCIAL

People with a preference for **Social** thinking are usually aware of the human dimension of whatever is taking place or is under discussion. They tend to be compassionate, empathic, intuitive about other people, and socially sensitive. They're the first to ask what effect a new company policy will have

on everyone, and they'll advocate for what is fair or for those who are not present. When speaking to people with this preference, provide more than just the facts. They like stories and prefer personal, uplifting words and conversations. They do not shy away from emotion, so support their passions. Be aware that they are sensitive and you might hurt their feelings. Ask them how they *feel* about whatever you are discussing, and let them know their opinion is valued. People with this preference value sincerity more than biting wit.

CONCEPTUAL

People with a preference for Conceptual thinking are usually so inventive and imaginative that you're at risk of losing their interest quickly. They have lively brains that want to play with ideas, implications, and tangents. They naturally think about the global view, the big picture, and long-term possibilities. They excel at breaking down  old barriers and coming up with creative new possibilities and solutions. People with this preference like things fun, whimsical, and futuristic instead of mundane and well-rehearsed. They prefer playful, inspirational words and conversations. They'll be more willing to listen if you use metaphors and give them a chance to fill in some blanks for themselves. Don't expect an answer right away – they need time to brainstorm and let new ideas surface. And don't bog them down with details – they won't listen anyway.

EXPRESSIVENESS

People at the quiet end of the **Expressiveness** spectrum are usually private and reserved. Although their brains are busy processing what you're saying, their facial expressions most likely will not change. Even if on the inside they have strong opinions about what's being discussed or find a conversation upsetting, they'll remain stoic. Most people with this preference will listen attentively but won't say anything unless you ask them directly. They prefer to process information internally in their own time. Find someplace out of earshot to talk and have a one-on-one, contemplative conversation. Think before you speak, be understated, use fewer words than usual (unless you have the same Profile), use a measured tone, and don't be alarmed if there are silences in the middle of your conversation. If you ask them to share their opinions before they are ready, this will create some tension.

People at the animated end of the **Expressiveness** spectrum are usually outgoing, talkative, and lively. They like exciting, dynamic words and conversations, and probably will need to move around as you speak. Don't be too reserved or you'll be steamrolled, albeit in the nicest possible way. People with this Profile are gregarious and extroverted, and don't shy away from group conversations – or even holding several conversations at once. They'll need to think things through with you out loud – and where they begin talking may not be where they end up.

ASSERTIVENESS

People at the peacekeeping end of the Assertiveness spectrum usually prefer amiable, cooperative, conciliatory conversations and words. They like a gentle, deliberate pace without confrontation or drama. No matter what they are thinking, they'll remain polite because they don't want to rock the boat under any circumstances. In a group, they'll appear neutral and hope that consensus will be built around your topic without the need for them to express their opinion. People with this Profile are so compliant that you'll need to ask for their opinion. Don't try to rush them.

People at the forceful end of the Assertiveness spectrum are usually driving and forceful. They like fast words and conversations that move things forward. They like having a lively debate, so be prepared to speak with vigor. They don't mind interruptions or a competitive environment. They don't have any hidden agendas and freely will share their opinions with you. Once they have decided that they like your solution, they will be ready to take action right away. It's always good to have people with this Profile on your side rather than working against you!

FLEXIBILITY

People at the focused end of the Flexibility spectrum are not looking for a lot of diverse options or open-ended discussions. They prefer precise words and conversations, with clear and cogent arguments that get to the point. People with this preference are usually open to change if you explain why it is necessary. They decide easily and will remain firm and steadfast in their opinion. They will listen for the implementation plan, and look for the line where discussing your topic turns into time to start working on it. Once they are set on a course of action, they want to see things through until completion. It's their way or the highway, so you won't have an easy time changing their mind.

People at the open-minded end of the Flexibility spectrum are usually affable and changeable. They accept ambiguity and believe that life is constantly changing. They're so open to possibilities that they don't mind changes, revisions, and interruptions. They don't care how they receive your information, but they do need time to weigh different options before settling on just one. If you have a pressing deadline and need a decision, give them as much time as you can but make it clear there's an end point.

THE UNIVERSAL LANGUAGE OF EMERGENETICS

The wonder of Emergenetics is that it provides a language that describes how people think and behave all over the world. It helps us understand ourselves and each other, whether we work side-by-side in a small business, or we are communicating between a sealed skyscraper in New York and an open bungalow in the tropics.

The following are three stories that illustrate how a mutual understanding of the Language of Grace eases conversations between diverse individuals and groups.

1. COOPERATION BETWEEN GLOBAL HEMISPHERES

A large, industrial corporation with divisions all over the world assigned a project to two teams, one in Bangalore, India, and the other

in New York City. Both teams spoke English, and both were composed of engineers who did highly technical work and had a great
deal of **Analytical** and Structural wiring in their brains – perfect
for what they did but not the easiest Profiles to merge together.
They were instructed to create a virtual team with cross-responsi-
bilities, working seamlessly together although they had never met,
were 8,300 miles apart, and the time in India is 9.5 hours ahead of
New York.

First, an Associate ran an Emergenetics Meeting of the Minds
workshop in New York, and the next day another Associate ran the
same workshop in India. All the participants were given the same
homework assignment, which was to download the Emergenetics
app onto their smartphones, connect with an individual across the
globe, and introduce themselves via Skype using the 3-2-1 exercise. In this case, they were instructed to look at the other person's
Emergenetics Profile and determine what they believed it indicated. (You also can use this exercise to explain your own Profile.)
They were to discuss:

3. Three points that aligned with that person's leadership style
2. Two points this individual needs to be aware of when working
   with others
1. The best way to communicate with this person.

Thus, each person was required to make educated guesses
about the other, based on the other person's Profile, and both individuals had an opportunity to discuss with each other how well
these assumptions held up. The feedback from the virtual team
was that they were extremely satisfied with the results. They got
to know each other and understand each other quickly, which
brought them to a greater level of productivity more rapidly than
anyone anticipated.

2. SUCCESS AT A FORTUNE 500 COMPANY

A large financial institution that serves a global market with over
9,000 employees who connect people and businesses in more

than 200 countries and territories was experiencing the following challenges:

1. Create the same workplace climate in its offices all over the world
2. Advance customer service in a similar way in 200 different countries and territories
3. Build a strengths-based corporate culture that would translate easily into so many different local cultures.

Their overall goal was to make sure each office was contributing to the parent company at a similar level. With such a large global workforce made up of so many individual workers, they recognized a need for greater consistency in training and development, plus improvements in the way employees interacted with each other and optimized their team successes.

This company chose Emergenetics to customize a full eLearning solution that would reach 3,000 employees. The program was vast in the numbers of participants and also comprehensive in the topics covered. It included Profiles for everyone, eLearning modules in key skill areas, uniform work tools, web-based learning, and huge webinars, as well as printed supplemental materials.

This coordinated eLearning effort was very successful. It introduced the universal language of Emergenetics throughout the company; improved employee performance; enabled better employee collaborations; reduced expenses for telecommunication and physical travel; and offered solutions for employee thinking, behavior, work styles and communication insights. Feedback indicated that 98% of their participants would recommend that peers and leaders enroll in the program, and they estimated that they saved over $500,000 in human resources consulting that was no longer needed.

3. CULTIVATING THE LANGUAGE OF GRACE

Cheryl Tang, a graduate student at National University of Singapore, wrote to us and said:

My teammates and I were conducting an overseas field study for Emergenetics in Shanghai, China. As part of the study, all 12 of us received our Emergenetics Profiles prior to the trip.

While on the trip, there were differing views on how we should scope and format our final deliverables. This resulted in lengthy meetings and ultimately conflict with one individual and a breakdown in communication. In a bid to make sense of things, we split up into smaller teams and discussed the possible reasons for the conflict and how to work around it.

What surprised me in the midst of all this was that, despite the breakdown in communication, there were no bad feelings involved. We unknowingly gravitated toward finding out about the Profile of the person we were conflicting with, and, using our knowledge of Emergenetics, tried to understand why the differences arose.

Several members were uncomfortable with one teammate's constantly saying, "This is the overview for now, we can work on the details later." They later realised it was not because he was too lazy to think of a structure for the final report; it was because his primary attribute is Conceptual thinking while his least preferred attribute is **Structural** thinking. This helped us understand him through his thinking preferences and hence made handling the conflict much easier.

REFLECTION

Different generations have been brought up with different attitudes, and the use of language is a large part of that. Your choice of words can help, heal, hurt, harm, or humiliate. If you are part of the older generation, you'll remember destructive statements that focus on deficiencies, such as "you're clumsy," "you're stupid," "you can't do math," "girls can't play football," "boys don't cry," and so on. Words are indeed powerful, and all it takes is one experience like this to color your entire life. On the other hand, many Millennials have been brought up with constructive language and phrases that encourage their strengths and spares their feelings, such as "just do your best," "you can do it if you practice," "you've always been good with numbers," or "different people are good at different things; you're fine the way you are." By starting with preferred attributes and the knowledge of how people prefer to think and behave, it's possible to build on their strengths rather than expecting them to become someone they're not.

IMPLEMENTATION STEPS

How do you begin creating a corporate culture that embraces gratitude?

1. First, be very aware of the words you choose. Start with how they affect you personally, which will heighten your sensitivity to how they affect others. Start by changing one habit; for example, say "I'm tied up with phone calls until 4:00 today" instead of "I'm busy!" Remember to use open-ended phrases ("We haven't made a billion dollars *yet.*") Be conscious of judgmental or value-laden words (very, high, not). Use words that enhance energy ("I lost" becomes "I didn't win this time," and "Try hard" becomes "Do your best").
2. Remember to keep other people's Profiles in mind and to use words and phrases that resonate with them. Also tailor your manner to their behavioral attributes. What one person regards as a bracing debate could crush someone else.
3. Obtain Emergenetics Profiles for everyone on your team (preferably everyone in your workplace) and have them uploaded to the Emergenetics app. This will give people the vocabulary they need to communicate positively with one another at their fingertips. It also will help embed the Language of Grace into your workplace. Be Sheryl and Penny. Before meeting with someone, review their Profile to make your conversation as productive as possible.

TEMPLATES FOR PRINCIPLE #3:
USING THE LANGUAGE OF GRACE

1. **HOW TO DELIVER A TOUGH MESSAGE**
   Rules are rules.

2. **HOW DIFFERENT ATTRIBUTES CALL A MEETING**
   One task done ten different ways

3. **HOW TO SPEAK TO DIFFERENT ATTRIBUTES**
   Using phrases others understand to make yourself understood

How To Deliver A Tough Message

Rules are rules.

F

A leader whose brain is primarily ANALYTICAL might say, "The policy states that employees will dress business casual. Please wear close-toed shoes."

A leader whose brain is primarily CONCEPTUAL might say, "I know that you pride yourself on being unique, but I challenge you to wear non-traditional, close-toed shoes in the office."

A leader whose brain is primarily STRUCTURAL might say, "I assume that you were unaware of the rules. Here is the handbook; you will notice that proper footwear is a close-toed shoe."

A leader whose brain is primarily SOCIAL might say, "I love the rhinestones on your flip-flops. Though they are in fashion, I am concerned for your safety, which is why I don't include flip-flops in the dress code."

E

A

A leader in the first third of EXPRESSIVENESS will most likely choose to send an email.

A leader in the third third of EXPRESSIVENESS might use humor to defuse any tension around the situation.

A leader in the first third of ASSERTIVENESS might say, "Are you aware of some of the details in our dress code?"

A leader in the third third of ASSERTIVENESS might explain the policy directly and point out that what the person is wearing is outside the policy.

A leader in the first third of FLEXIBILITY would most likely point out the policy in a focused manner, without mincing words.

A leader in the third third of FLEXIBILITY might say, "There are a variety of options you might consider that will align with our policy."

Important Note: None of these attributes stand alone, but rather thread together in a way that produces WEteam magic.

How Different Attributes Call A Meeting

One task done 10 different ways.

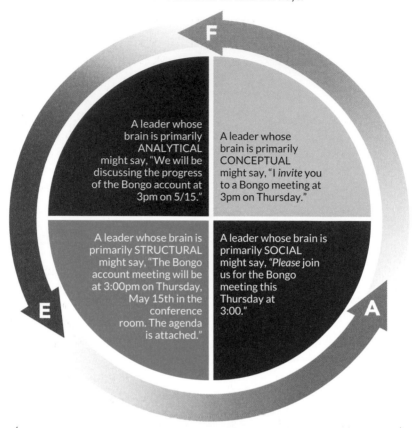

F

A leader whose brain is primarily ANALYTICAL might say, "We will be discussing the progress of the Bongo account at 3pm on 5/15."

A leader whose brain is primarily CONCEPTUAL might say, "I *invite* you to a Bongo meeting at 3pm on Thursday."

A leader whose brain is primarily STRUCTURAL might say, "The Bongo account meeting will be at 3:00pm on Thursday, May 15th in the conference room. The agenda is attached."

A leader whose brain is primarily SOCIAL might say, "*Please* join us for the Bongo meeting this Thursday at 3:00."

E

A

A leader in the first third of EXPRESSIVENESS might say, "Come to the meeting."

A leader in the third third of EXPRESSIVENESS might say, "We are so excited to get together."

A leader in the first third of ASSERTIVENESS might say, "Consider coming to the meeting."

A leader in the third third of ASSERTIVENESS might say, "Be at the meeting!"

A leader in the first third of FLEXIBILITY might say, "The Bongo meeting is scheduled for 3:00pm on the dot, this Thursday, no exceptions."

A leader in the third third of FLEXIBILITY might say, "I hope you are all available for a Bongo meeting at either 1:00 or 3:00pm on Monday or Thursday."

Important Note: None of these attributes stand alone, but rather thread together in a way that produces WEteam magic.

How to Speak to Different Attributes

Using phrases others understand to make yourself understood.

F

When speaking to the ANALYTICAL brain, you might say: "Let's cut to the chase." "What's the bottom line?" "What is the cost/benefit ratio?" "Let's explore this subject in depth."

When speaking to the CONCEPTUAL brain, you might say: "Let's not rein ourselves in." "How does this connect to the vision?" "This has the right flow." "Can we be globally assigned?"

When speaking to the STRUCTURAL brain, you might say: "We've always done it this way." "If it ain't broke, don't fix it." "Slow down, let's take this one step at a time." "What does the policy say?"

When speaking to the SOCIAL brain, you might say: "How do you feel about this?" "How will this affect your customers?" "Let's work through this together." "I'm hurt. You haven't returned my phone call from yesterday."

E

A

When speaking to those in the first third of EXPRESSIVENESS, you might say: "I'll give you time to process" or "Do you have anything to share?"

When speaking to those in the third third of EXPRESSIVENESS, you might say: "Let's talk this out" or "What are your initial thoughts?"

When speaking to those in the first third of ASSERTIVENESS, you might say: "Take your time" or "Let's see what the whole group has to say and get everyone on board."

When speaking to those in the third third of ASSERTIVENESS, you might say: "Jump right in and share your opinions!" or "Thank you for helping us drive this forward."

When speaking to those in the first third of FLEXIBILITY, you might say: "Let's stay the course" or "I appreciate you helping us stay focused."

When speaking to those in the third third of FLEXIBILITY, you might say: "Let's explore all the options" or "Thank you for your accommodating attitude."

Important Note. None of these attributes stand alone, but rather thread together in a way that produces WEteam magic.

CREATING A MEETING OF THE MINDS

WEteam Cognitive Collaboration

I don't have a problem with meetings. Research has shown that the collective intelligence of a group is greater than the intelligence of any one member of the group. But I do have a problem with how meetings are usually held.

I've attended meetings all over the world, and in my experience they're largely the same, whether I'm in Singapore or Sioux Falls. At an assigned hour, people drop their work, gather in a conference room, and exchange pleasantries. Sometimes high-carbohydrate snacks like bagels or muffins are on a side table. Except for the chairperson, every face in the room shows the same expression: "Why am I here, and how am I going to contribute?" Many people today are being asked to do twice the work in half the time, and a badly run meeting is an anathema. An agenda is passed out, a scribe and timekeeper are selected, and the most important person in the room outlines the topic that will absorb everyone's time for the next two hours.

Some people are at this meeting because they always have been. Division meetings are usually composed of managers above a certain job level. Company meetings are usually composed of executives from each division. But what guarantee is there that selecting people by the length of their experience at the company or by their job title is the most effective way to get things done?

This chapter is about the *real* key to productive teams, which is cognitive diversity. This is not simply a matter of putting diverse individuals of different ages, ethnicities, genders, and job levels in a room together. Research shows that this kind of diversity – which largely is based on whatever external factors we can see – predicts nothing about the success of a team.

When we talk about *cognitive collaboration* at Emergenetics, our approach is unlike any other. We Emergineer our meetings by bringing together people with the different Emergenetics attributes, not just different approaches or job titles. We base our teams on Emergenetics Profiles, which under the best circumstances allow us to predict the thinking and behavioral attributes of the team members in advance. When representatives of every attribute are present, we call this a Whole Emergenetics team, or *WEteam*. When you put a WEteam together, you can do anything. We use this technique both with clients and within the company because it's the fastest, most creative, and most reliable way I know to do work that works.

WEteams achieve a state of peak performance by creating synergy among all the Emergenetics attributes. These teams have the potential to collaborate at the highest level. By accessing all the different attributes in the room with mutual respect, team members communicate more clearly, are more creative, and come up with superior solutions more quickly.

Sometimes I liken the Power of WE to electricity. Behind every electrical outlet is a source of untapped energy. The outlet itself is the portal to that energy. If nothing is plugged in, then the energy waits inside the electric wiring, invisible and dormant, a power source that's never engaged. It remains potentially helpful but untapped. In teams and groups of people, there also is energy in the combined brilliances of all the Emergenetics attributes. If you can't correctly connect to that energy, it remains latent. The challenge that most teams have is figuring out how to tap into their own unique Power of WE.

Ideally, all the members of a WEteam are given a copy of their Profile to better understand how they think and behave. They also see each other's Profiles to better understand each other. Sharing Profiles:

- Allows team members to rapidly exchange relevant information about each other
- Encourages mutual understanding and the creation of a safe space where everyone feels empowered to speak up
- Jump-starts the meeting to a higher level of trust

- Sets up a creative dynamic among the different attributes, which both challenge and complement each other
- Surfaces the best ideas more quickly
- Helps people work together more productively
- Ensures team members will plan the optimal next steps, taking into account the priorities and expertise of each member of the team
- Shortens the amount of time spent in the meeting.

Let me give you an example.

DEMONSTRATING THE POWER OF A WEteam

It's not uncommon for companies to hire outside consultants to help them craft their mission statements. The consultant has done this many times before and often brings a perspective and expertise that an in-house employee can't provide – even the CEO.

I worked with the management team of a large gourmet food company to capture their goals for the next five years on paper and then fold all of them together into a mission statement. We had two days and a team of 17 people to accomplish this task – although on the first day, only 16 people showed up.

The CEO said, "Oh, we can start the meeting without Nadia. She is an executive assistant and her presence is not crucial for this meeting."

The members of the team had taken the Emergenetics questionnaire ahead of time, and I had all their Profiles – and they did, too. The thinking style of the CEO was **Analytical** and Conceptual, and the rest of the team had various combinations of **Analytical**, **Structural**, and Conceptual thinking.

I was going to point out why Nadia's presence was indeed important, but I did not want to directly contradict the CEO right off the bat, so I decided to wait and let the importance of Nadia's absence become apparent on its own.

The Profile of the entire group looked like this:

TEAM PROFILE GOURMET FOOD COMPANY

EMERGENETICS® | GROUP

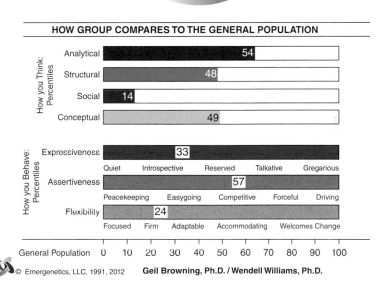

XYZ CORPORATION
HOW YOU THINK: PERCENTAGES

ANALYTICAL = 37%
- Clear thinker
- Logical problem solver
- Enjoys math
- Rational
- Learns by mental analysis

CONCEPTUAL = 28%
- Imaginative
- Intuitive about ideas
- Visionary
- Enjoys the unusual
- Learns by experimenting

STRUCTURAL = 27%
- Practical thinker
- Likes guidelines
- Cautious of new ideas
- Predictable
- Learns by doing

SOCIAL = 8%
- Intuitive about people
- Socially aware
- Relational
- Empathic
- Learns from others

HOW GROUP COMPARES TO THE GENERAL POPULATION

How you Think: Percentiles		
Analytical	54	
Structural	48	
Social	14	
Conceptual	49	

How you Behave: Percentiles					
Expressiveness	33				
	Quiet	Introspective	Reserved	Talkative	Gregarious
Assertiveness	57				
	Peacekeeping	Easygoing	Competitive	Forceful	Driving
Flexibility	24				
	Focused	Firm	Adaptable	Accommodating	Welcomes Change

General Population 0   10   20   30   40   50   60   70   80   90   100

© Emergenetics, LLC, 1991, 2012   **Geil Browning, Ph.D. / Wendell Williams, Ph.D.**

Overall, they didn't mind talking about their ideas (**Expressiveness**), they liked moving things forward (Assertiveness), and they tended to have strong opinions (Flexibility).

Making a point of using positive words and the Language of Grace, we worked for a few hours and developed a list of goals for the company that satisfied everyone. It looked like this:

1. Increase our profits by 30% for the fiscal year.
2. Update our data center technology.
3. Evaluate and streamline our processes for production.
4. Develop a timeline for rolling out new company-wide policies.
5. Take our company to a new level by expanding our distributorship around the world.
6. Work in a quiet atmosphere but a fast-paced environment.
7. Drive to succeed and be committed to brilliant execution.

Then we worked out an initial mission statement, which looked like this:

> Super Yummy Corporation has become the number one gourmet foods company in the nation by providing quality products at a reasonable price. We use effective and efficient administration of services, while we expand our distributorships around the world, creating profits for our shareholders.

Finally, I took out a blank Emergenetics template, and we went through the goals one a time, putting each one inside the applicable attribute on the template. The first two goals would best be accomplished by people with a lot of **Analytical** thinking in their brains. The next two goals fell into the **Structural** section of the template. The global goal went to the Conceptual thinkers. The "quiet atmosphere" was easily assigned to the **Expressive** attribute, the "drive to succeed" was associated with Assertiveness, and the "brilliant execution" was aligned with Flexibility. The template looked like this:

GOALS FOR GOURMET FOOD COMPANY
SORTED INTO TEMPLATE

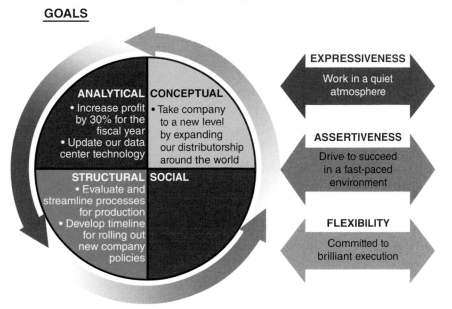

It was obvious to all the members of the team that the spot for the **Social** attribute was empty. I pointed out that the mission statement had no reference to their end users – the customers who would buy their products.

The CEO said, "Well, of course we are thinking about the customers. It's implied in the statement. Why do we need to write it down?" We wrapped up the meeting on this note, and I deliberately let the question hang until the next day.

When we reconvened, Nadia was able to attend. The CEO was not especially interested in stopping our progress to hear the contribution of an executive assistant, but I made a point of handing a copy of the mission statement to Nadia and asking her what she thought.

Nadia said, "Well, I like it. But it seems a little cold. Why haven't you put in anything about our customers?"

The room fell silent. Nadia had the missing **Social** attribute in her brain, as well as a great deal of experience speaking to customers (**Expressiveness**) and an attitude of deference to them – "the customer is always right" (Flexibility). In fact, customers were the first thing she thought of.

We spent the next hour revising the statement.

The executive team ended the meeting early with an excellent mission statement. In addition to becoming fans of the Emergenetics Profile, they also learned:

- Write everything out.
- Use positive words.
- Assume everyone else has different priorities than you do.
- Avoid being judgmental about anyone else's attributes.
- Have someone representing *every attribute* at *every meeting*.

A WEteam usually does not just fall together naturally. You need to assemble the correct people to get a complete array of thinking and behavioral attributes. The ways to make this happen are discussed next.

WE ARE WIRED TO COLLABORATE

Our brains are wired for collaborating, which is one reason WEteams are so successful. Long before researchers proved it using MRIs, Aristotle noted that "Man is by nature a social animal," and John Donne famously said, "No man is an island." The brain is inherently social. It's common knowledge that people who are part of a group are happier, healthier, and more resilient than people who are isolated and alone.

Human beings have outsized brains compared to other species. The size of our neocortex is unusually large. Anthropologist Robin Dunbar found that, although the size of the brains of most species seems to be related to the size of the animal, body size is not the determining factor. It turns out that the strongest predictor of brain size is the size of an animal's social group. We have big brains in order to socialize.

It makes a difference with whom we socialize. For better or for worse, we are wired to take on the values and goals of our group. When we work together as a fully functioning team, such as a WEteam, we not only take on the priorities of the group but also feed the desire of our brains to be included and contribute our unique talents.

CREATING A WEteam FOR COGNITIVE COLLABORATION

WEteams take some thought because they're not based on simple concepts like job titles or IQ or expertise alone. The goal is to effectively harness the power of cognitive diversity, which means putting together people who might not otherwise even talk to each other. What's the most efficient way to do that?

CREATE A COMPANY CULTURE OF TRUST

Your company culture can either support or undermine WEteams. If you're the leader of the company, your responsibility is to provide the culture that allows the brilliance of each attribute to come forth. This topic is mentioned many times throughout this book, but in short: use positive words and the Language of Grace; allow people to fail forward; believe in each of your employees; honor everyone's attributes; encourage collaboration rather than competition; and allow people to work without fear or judgment. When you start with employees who already are operating at a high level of cooperation, your WEteam will reach a place of trust and the honest exchange of ideas more easily.

HIRE FOR COMPETENCE

People need to be able to do what you're asking them to do. To form a high-functioning WEteam at your company, you need to be able to draw from a pool of employees who are both competent and diverse. Obviously incompetent people aren't going to be very helpful, and research has proved that diversity alone does not ensure better team results.

People often want to use the Emergenetics Profile for hiring, but I'm asking you to guard against doing that. It doesn't test for competence. We do use the Profile as *part* of the onboarding process, and for our new hires we keep it on hand so that later we can use it to form cognitively diverse teams.

At Emergenetics, we hire for competence, and we measure it through the Emergenetics Selection Program (ESP). That includes the job analysis in which we set desired results for a position and predict on-the-job performance needs. The result of the job analysis is a clear depiction of the workplace motivators (interests, preferences, attitudes) and required aptitudes (skills) for any given role. Once candidates complete the ESP assessment, you can quickly and easily see how any individual compares to the role's requirements. Based on a candidate's ESP results, questions can be tailored to uncover greater insights into workplace preferences. The combination of scientific evidence and the behavioral interview empowers the hiring team to make the right hire, every time. The ESP will prevent you from hiring that charming, collegial candidate who doesn't actually have much to offer. You must be willing to hire, work with, and promote people who are not like you, people who even make you uncomfortable but bring exceptional quality to your group.

Hire people who want to keep learning. It's not necessary for the employee to be on fire with ambition to reach the C-level, but every worker should be willing to engage in some form of continuous learning. The willingness to feel scratchy about skills and knowledge is a must.

An employee is not like a spark plug you can replace at any time with an identical spark plug. Instead of looking for new spark plugs that fit into the corporate machine, change your corporate culture around your competent new hires who will contribute in their own brilliant way. Discover how they like to learn. Find out about their ambitions and what they like to do – and craft their job so they can progress toward that goal. When you find good employees, it benefits your company to help them advance and retain them as their skills increase. Take a unique approach to each one. Invest in keeping your good workers instead of replacing them. The more you Emergineer your corporation, the more your employees will trust you, the happier they will be, and the more you will reap the benefits I mentioned under Centering on page 45 – like your workers having 106% more energy and feeling 76% more engagement.

BEWARE BIASES

People who speak, think, behave, and sometimes even dress in similar ways tend to be comfortable with each other and gather together. There's a reason the "old boy network" has survived for hundreds of years. Uniformity is one of the worst things management can allow to happen. Hire for diversity, not comfort.

You may unconsciously make assumptions or use stereotypes. For example, you may naturally gravitate to, or away from, the following kinds of people:

- Do you believe you are more gifted than the people below you?
- How do you react to people who ask about your weekend plans?
- How do you react to people who try to keep the meeting on time?
- Do you assume that all women have a preference for **Social** thinking and that all men have a preference for **Analytical** thinking?
- What do you think of people who will not move ahead until there is undisputed data available?
- What do you think of people who don't follow the timelines on agendas?
- How much do you think "creatives" add to a team?
- What do you think of people who push their favorite solution vigorously?
- What are your thoughts about people who prefer not to speak unless spoken to?

Debiasing is now a thing, for good reason. Some professors overcome their personal biases by having an assistant cover up the name of the student who wrote each paper before grading them. And after orchestras began holding auditions behind a screen – so the gender of the musician was not known – female membership shot up from 5% in 1970 to almost 40% today.

Even under the best of circumstances, we all have certain biases. Leaders who are stressed, exhausted, worried, or even hungry are more likely to fall back on theirs. When that happens, they may think they're being more open-minded than they really are. Hungry or not, Emergenetics hiring practices and the Emergenetics template are their best friends.

BEWARE GROUPTHINK

If you assemble a group in which everyone has the same preferences, there will be very little creative push-and-pull. A roomful of quiet people might sit in relative silence, or a roomful of talkative people might get louder and louder as they try to speak over each other. In one study, different groups were given a challenge to solve within a limited amount of time. The most cognitively diverse team solved the challenge in 21 minutes. The roomful of IT experts never finished at all. They all were determined to solve the problem in their own heads; they never collaborated; and nothing was accomplished.

Another potential problem with a team that lacks diversity is that all the members will go down the same path and create that enemy of creativity: *groupthink*. Many dying companies are filled with extremely smart, driven people. Why would such bright people go wrong? They may have succumbed to groupthink.

The interesting aspect of groupthink is that the information each group needs to make a course correction easily is available. They don't need to look for an obscure fact or equation or miracle. They simply need to open their eyes to the ways in which other people think and behave.

HERE'S HOW DIFFERENT ATTRIBUTES CONTRIBUTE TO YOUR WEteam

It's difficult to see all the subtleties at first, but after 25 years of working with many thousands of company employees and workshop participants, my associates and I have made observations about how people prefer to think and behave. These tendencies have remained stable for a long time, for all kinds of people.

Imagine there's a roomful of workshop participants who have been separated into smaller groups by preferences. Here's how they report the way they prefer to work.

THE BEHAVIORAL ATTRIBUTES

FIRST-THIRD EXPRESSIVENESS

If you put a group of FIRST-THIRD EXPRESSIVES together and ask them about how they complete tasks, they will report:

1. "We are comfortable with silence."
2. "I have plenty of thoughts going on in my head, but you won't know it."
3. "When we ultimately speak, we have considered all the options."

The nonverbals of this group are subtle. They use precise words and maintain a calm appearance. They would tell you that they're good listeners, only speak when necessary, and keep a poker face so they can keep their cards close to their vest.

When asked about the process in their group, they will report: "We like being in this group. It took a while before we got started, but when we did, it was easy. No one talked over us. "

When asked, "Would you like to work in a group of people with only first-third **Expressiveness**?" their answer might be, "No, I would like it for a short time, but eventually, it would be tiring. I prefer it when I don't have to carry the conversation. I don't want to be constantly put on the spot to say something."

THIRD-THIRD EXPRESSIVENESS

If you put a group of **THIRD-THIRD EXPRESSIVES** together and ask them about how they complete tasks, they will report:

1. "We bring energy to the group."
2. "People always know what we're thinking."
3. "We draw people out and fill the silence in the room."

You almost always know what's happening by the looks on their faces and their larger-than-life mannerisms. You hear their entire train of thought, and you may think that their first sentences have encapsulated their ideas, but they're just getting started. Thoughts in their head now are coming out of their mouths.

When asked about the process in their group, they'll report: "What fun it was to be in this group. We all talked at the same time and no one was offended and we all understood what each person was saying. It was exciting!"

If you ask, "Would you like to work in a group of people with only **THIRD-THIRD EXPRESSIVENESS**?" their answer will be, "No, I'd like it for a short time, but eventually it would be tiring because no one is listening to me and everyone is talking over each other. If we had differing opinions, no one would take the time to see another perspective because we all would be too busy advocating for our own ideas!"

Everyone has a degree of Assertiveness. The difference between first thirds and third thirds is in how they show it.

FIRST-THIRD ASSERTIVENESS

FIRST-THIRD ASSERTIVES tend to influence others by asking questions. For example, they might ask, "What do you think about adding Roger Brown to the team?" This question is like taking the temperature of the group. It encourages others to voice their agreement or concerns. The responses will indicate who is aligned with adding Roger to the team, and who needs to be influenced. The FIRST-THIRD ASSERTIVES make no outward signs of distress.

If you put a group of FIRST-THIRD ASSERTIVES together and ask them about how they complete tasks, they will report:

1. "We make our case without creating conflict."
2. "We don't rush into things."
3. "We are willing to compromise."

THIRD-THIRD ASSERTIVENESS

This is a much gentler approach than that of the THIRD-THIRD ASSERTIVES, who will just say, "Add Roger Brown to the team," and wait for the dissent that follows. When that happens, you immediately get a clear understanding of how the group feels about adding Roger to the team. This approach relies on debate – which makes the first thirds uncomfortable, so you may not get their true opinions.

If you put a group of THIRD-THIRD ASSERTIVES together and ask them about how they complete tasks, they will report:

1. "We embrace confrontation."
2. "We help others express their views."
3. "We are hard-charging."

Everyone has FLEXIBILITY. The difference between first thirds and third thirds is in how they use it.

FIRST-THIRD FLEXIBILITY

It is important to understand that FIRST-THIRD FLEXIBLES like considering options as much as the third thirds, but they are even more energized by executing a project, so making a decision is more important to them than *talking* about making one. For them, constantly going off course feels like moving backward. The gift of those in the first third is their "why?" questions in times of change, such as, "will making this alteration benefit the outcome?" They also might ask, "Is this just a new idea that the third third will want to change later because of a dream in the middle of the night?"

If you put a group of FIRST-THIRD FLEXIBLES together and ask them about how they complete tasks, they will report:

1. "We keep the team on point."
2. "We are laser-focused."
3. "We are decisive."

THIRD-THIRD FLEXIBILITY

THIRD-THIRD FLEXIBLES prefer to consider options before a final decision is made, and they believe information that comes to them in the middle of the night is perfectly valid. For them, life without ongoing possibilities and options is stifling. Ultimately this dance between the first thirds and third thirds ends up benefiting the overall project or work being accomplished.

If you put a group of THIRD-THIRD FLEXIBLES together and ask them about how they complete tasks, they will report:

1. "We cope well if changes happen at the last minute."
2. "We are energized when options are open."
3. "Decisions are a working draft."

Because the dynamic between the FIRST-THIRD FLEXIBLES and the THIRD-THIRD FLEXIBLES is so important, it can be an issue if your group has *only* first thirds or *only* third thirds. If only first thirds are available, they may not agree with the outcome and may want to stick to their own opinions. If only third thirds are available, they will speak up to advocate their own ideas, but they aren't exactly sure what they are. Often they can't land on one idea and then stick with it. In the end the third thirds *might* come to consensus, but it will take longer.

THE THINKING ATTRIBUTES

Here are the most common combinations of thinking attributes that thread together, and how they report their brilliance.

CONVERGENT

When you put a group of Convergent (**Analytical**/**Structural**) thinkers together and ask them how they prefer to complete a task, they will say:

1. "We read the instructions."
2. "We analyze how we want to proceed."
3. "We brainstorm on a piece of paper, and then transfer the results to the final sheet used in the report."

When asked where they like to work, the answer is generally, "We prefer to be seated around a table." If time is a factor, someone is responsible for making sure that the work is completed efficiently. When asked, "How much did you laugh, and how many side conversations did you have?," the response is likely, "No laughter and no side conversations until the task is complete." Which is why they complete tasks on time or preferably early. These brains usually keep everyone on task.

On the other hand, if you put a group of Divergent (**Social/** Conceptual) thinkers together and ask them how they prefer to complete a task, they will say:

DIVERGENT

1. "First we get caught up. I need to find out about your weekend activities, or your boyfriend's new job, or your new goldendoodle."
2. "We brainstorm by drawing ideas, making sure we have a variety of colored markers. We prefer the scented magic markers, and we may have to sniff them first and tell stories about how we used them as children."
3. "Our process includes a ping-pong of ideas, until we land on just the perfect result."

When asked where they work, response is weather dependent. "If the weather is nice we prefer to be outdoors. Being in a windowless room stifles our process. Time is optional – after all, man invented time." When asked, "How much did you laugh?," the response is, "The entire time. Laughter is our best friend. This freedom of expression unleashes our creativity, resulting in a better outcome."

When you put a group of Abstract (**Analytical/** Conceptual) thinkers together and ask them how they prefer to complete a task, they will say:

ABSTRACT

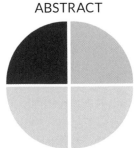

1. "Give me the reason why we have to do this, and if the reason is valid enough, we will research the most efficient way to complete the project."
2. "We will use a logical approach and emphasize the big picture, ultimately focusing on the overall outcome."

3. "In the end, we know our conclusions are right." (This is not **As-**
   sertiveness dependent. The **Analytical**/Conceptual part of the
   brain has great faith in its intellectual abilities.)

Note that nothing is said about any of the details of the project, and nothing is said about people. When this group does speak
about people, it is always in terms of teams, or the person who can
help accomplish the task, and not about the individuals.

When you put a group of Concrete (**Structural**/**Social**) thinkers
together and ask them how they prefer to complete a task, they
will say:

1. "We get together as a group first and
   check in."
2. "Together we ask, 'What is the task and
   what are the guidelines?'"
3. "We make a list of what we need to accomplish. Each person takes an item
   from the list and accomplishes it independently until it is perfect. In the end,
   we get together again to validate the accomplishments of each team member, and then we present the
   final project together."

Note that nothing is said about the "why" of the project or the
vision.

It is helpful to know how each attribute thinks, but remember
this is just the start of a WEteam. Separately, each of these groups
provides adequate work, but when members of each group are put
together, their combined brilliance takes creativity and productivity up another notch.

AM I FINISHED YET?

No. After you have put your WEteam members together, each of
whom represents at least one Emergenetics attribute, you are still
not done. It isn't enough to put a selection of smart, competent,

cognitively diverse people in a room together. Why not? Putting this crowd together can be scratchy. At this moment, they are like people who live on different planets, and the conversation may be full of intent/impact gaps.

You need to add one more brain: a multi-modal thinker who helps translate the vocabulary and ideas from one thinking attribute to another. Multi-modal thinkers are able to facilitate communication to avoid misunderstandings, dropped stitches, hurt feelings, or tempers flaring. For example, when the person with the most **Structural** thinking says that the group has run five minutes over its allotted time for Topic C, the team member who was just speaking could easily take this personally. ("Is she telling me to shut up?") The facilitator can gently point out that the **Structural** brain was simply doing what it does best. When the person with the most Conceptual thinking offers a farfetched idea, others might be quick to pounce, unless the facilitator reminds everyone that this is what the Conceptual brain does best, and perhaps others could try to see merit in the idea.

FACILITATOR

A good team facilitator will also understand how the different behavioral attributes interact. A very quiet person (**Expressiveness**) does not want to be put on the spot, but a very animated person (**Expressiveness**) needs to talk. The facilitator may occasionally need to encourage one while calming down the other.

The template at the end of this chapter called *Overall Team Dynamics Among Attributes* condenses helpful information about how the different behavioral attributes balance each other, as well as what each thinking attribute brings to the table, and how they all support and challenge each other. When the group values its collective diversity, the meeting will generate creative tension. The best leaders pay attention to what they do to encourage this kind of synergy. If this group understands the Language of Grace, they will create a positive energetic tension that produces an innovative solution in a short period of time.

ASSEMBLE YOUR TEAM MEMBERS

SAMPLE WEteam

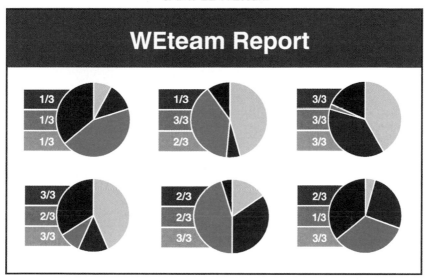

Now that it's time to create your WEteam, you have a variety of competent, self-aware people to consider who already are inclined to trust each other because your company climate is one of mutual respect. Aim for a group of five to eight people who, taken together, represent different attributes of Emergenetics. Remember, most people have one or more thinking preferences, and when you consider both ends of the behavioral spectrum there are six different behaviors (plus the It Depends category). If you have more than eight people, the group ultimately subdivides into smaller groups which may not be useful.

If these people are all your employees, or if they include clients with whom you are doing Emergenetics training, you will already have their Profiles on hand. Making sure every attribute is present requires studying each Profile and balancing the team overall. This is fascinating work, but it can be time-consuming. The easiest thing to do is to train someone in your office to assemble WEteams by looking at the Profiles of different prospective team members.

When you assemble your WEteam, do not worry excessively about expertise. It is important to bring in not only people who are knowledgeable in the content being discussed, but also people who are experts in their Profile and in the attributes. If you are putting a team together to build a rocket ship to the moon, you need an engineer or two on the team. However, you also need a brain that thinks differently to add different energy to the group. Maybe, for example, you might want to add a musician, or an artist, or your administrative assistant. These people may not know anything about engineering, but they will bring a different point of view to the issue. They can add amazing richness to the team. They will come up with something, even if they use the wrong terms, or they will ask questions that will shake up the assumptions of the others.

People are entirely too quick to pass on this idea, saying, "Why would I ever bring anybody into this team who is not an expert?" They are worried that this might reflect poorly on them, or that the person might make a fool of themselves, or other staff will be resentful, and so on. Our belief is that, provided the leader frames the situation correctly, the benefits of bringing in this different perspective outweigh the risks.

WHAT DOES EACH ATTRIBUTE NEED FOR PSYCHOLOGICAL SAFETY IN A TEAM?

As a leader, your first goal is to establish trust among your WEteam members. If people are afraid of being ridiculed, they will play it safe and not offer up their ideas. A good beginning is to have each member of the team share some information about themselves, based on their Profile. We use a 3-2-1 exercise in which everybody introduces themselves, shares something insightful about their Profile, and says something about how they prefer to be spoken to. For example:

3. Here are three points that align with my leadership style.
2. Here are two points of my Profile that I need to be aware of when working with others.
1. What is the best way to communicate with me?

After this step, posting all the Profiles further establishes transparency, and allows people to see who shares their preferred attributes and who does not. It helps a great deal to understand that while Percival seems a little arrogant, it's just because he has a "brilliant brain" with **Analytical**/**Structural**/Conceptual preferences and honestly believes he is smarter than everyone else in the room. Letitia hasn't spoken a word, but that's because she is in the first third of all the behavioral attributes, and she will speak when she is ready – or after enough time has elapsed and someone asks her to. Dwayne can be heard telling stories and joking as he walks down the hall toward the conference room. He is in the third third of **Expressiveness** and loves being the life of a party. All of these people are simply thinking and behaving the way they were innately wired, and – provided they all have good intentions – nothing they say or do in the meeting should be taken personally.

It is the team leader's job to clearly explain the challenge for the meeting. Different thinking attributes hear things differently, so the goal should be stated in several ways to make sure everyone understands it.

Some housekeeping will help establish a sense of order:

- Remind everyone to be on time.
- Explain that each meeting will start with a few minutes of centering, so it is essential that everyone show up as requested.
- Always provide an agenda – preferably in advance.
- Also provide written information in advance for the benefit of people who have a preference for **Analytical** or Structural thinking.
- Assign a timekeeper. When this person calls attention to the time during the meeting, remember that is the part of the job.
- Assign a scribe or note-taker.

Next, establish that this meeting will be a safe place. Everybody will:

- Use the Language of Grace.
- Let others be themselves.
- Appreciate each other's gifts and unique talents.
- Remember that all Profiles are perfect.

- Value the Other (complementary profiles).
- Block their biases.
- Recall that mistakes are learning opportunities, not opportunities for criticism.
- Refrain from interrupting another team member while he/she is speaking.
- Pull their own weight.
- Give their reasoning when they disagree.
- Provide only the best data, and verify their assumptions before speaking.

In addition to these general recommendations, there are attribute-specific norms to keep in mind. Please refer to these two templates at the end of this chapter:

1. What Does Each Attribute Need for Psychological Safety on a Team?
2. What Norms (Ground Rules) Does Each Attribute Need?

REFLECTION

Company success is always due to the kind of people you have in your company, *plus* the way they are encouraged. The first part is accomplished by hiring competent workers and building teams from people who do not think or behave in the same way. The second part comes from appreciating their differences and trusting them to use their gifts for the good of the cause. You can't build an orchestra with nothing but oboes. When you surround an oboe with a clarinet, bassoon, flute, piccolo, and every other instrument, then you have an orchestra. When you encourage all of these musicians to listen to each other and to work harmoniously together, then you have music.

IMPLEMENTATION STEPS

1. Do an analysis of your team – is it cognitively diverse? If so, are you tapping in to that diversity? If not, what's missing? Identify which preferences are not represented, and which attributes may be under or over represented to drive toward a balanced and complete approach.
2. If there is a missing attribute, invite someone to your meeting/ project/event who has a preference in that attribute.
3. Provide a safe environment in which everyone can exercise their brilliance.

TEMPLATES FOR PRINCIPLE #4: *CREATING A MEETING OF THE MINDS*

1. **OVERALL TEAM DYNAMICS AMONG ATTRIBUTES**
   How do the different attributes interact in a meeting?

2. **WHAT DOES EACH ATTRIBUTE NEED FOR PSYCHOLOGICAL SAFETY ON A TEAM?**
   Psychological safety begins with vulnerability and trust.

3. **WHAT NORMS (GROUND RULES) DOES EACH ATTRIBUTE NEED?**
   How to honor the uniqueness of each attribute

The Overall Team Dynamics Among Attributes

How do the different attributes interact in a meeting?

F

ANALYTICAL thinkers may bring data to the table. They can be counted on to gather information, to do outside research and to consider solutions from different angles.

CONCEPTUAL thinkers may bring unusual ideas to the table. They will likely look at the big picture, see creative opportunities and wait for a solution to surface in their minds. They usually prefer a non-typical environment and meetings that involve brainstorming.

STRUCTURAL thinkers may bring a timeline to the table. They may remember important details, consider what rules and constraints exist, weigh risks and consequences and design a plan with appropriate milestones. Agendas sent out ahead of time are a must!

SOCIAL thinkers may bring the relational aspect to the table. They will likely prefer a collaborative approach, consider how different solutions will affect others and ultimately make a decision by consulting others and using their gut instinct.

E

A

Those in the first third of EXPRESSIVENESS may prefer time to think before speaking and would rather not be called on without having prior notice.

Those in the third third of EXPRESSIVENESS may get the group going and continue to speak while others may be thinking.

Those in the first third of ASSERTIVENESS may provide a calming influence in times of debate and conflict.

Those in the third third of ASSERTIVENESS may want to openly challenge ideas in order for the best thoughts to rise to the top.

Those in the first third of FLEXIBILITY may balance the people at the other end of the spectrum by pushing for an ultimate decision.

Those in the third third of FLEXIBILITY are most likely interested in knowing that any aspect of a decision can be reevaluated at any point of the project or meeting.

Important Note: None of these attributes stand alone, but rather thread together in a way that produces WEteam magic.

What Does Each Attribute Need For Psychological Safety On A Team?

Psychological safety begins with vulnerability and trust.

F

ANALYTICAL thinkers may need accurate information and to feel like they can trust the abilities of the other team members. They will also likely need the freedom to ask questions.

CONCEPTUAL thinkers may need the freedom to share their ideas without judgment. They also may need to trust that they can take risks and try new things.

STRUCTURAL thinkers may need others to respect time constraints. They may also need a clear understanding of their role in the group. They will likely need to trust that the other team members will also honor time commitments.

SOCIAL thinkers may need to talk about something from outside work. They may also need to feel that the other team members care about their well-being and will likely need to be able to trust the group with the information they share.

E

A

Team members in the first third of EXPRESSIVENESS may need some moments of quiet, even if that means taking a break. They may also need to trust that they have time to process their thoughts internally.

Team members in the third third of EXPRESSIVENESS may need the freedom to express initial ideas that may change. They may need to trust that they can process their thoughts out loud.

Team members in the first third of ASSERTIVENESS may need to trust that the team has a common goal. They may also need to trust that they can be silent until asked for an opinion.

Team members in the third third of ASSERTIVENESS may need to debate. They may also need to trust that they can offer their ideas until a decision is made.

Team members in the first third of FLEXIBILITY may need to trust that they have the freedom to stay focused on completing the task at hand.

Team members in the third third of FLEXIBILITY may need to trust that they have the freedom to thoroughly consider different points of view.

Important Note: None of these attributes stand alone, but rather thread together in a way that produces WEteam magic.

What Norms (Ground Rules) Does Each Attribute Need?

How to honor the uniqueness of each attribute.

F

People whose brains are largely ANALYTICAL will likely need to know their time will not be wasted by team members who bluff or bring poor data.

People whose brains are largely CONCEPTUAL will likely need a safe space in which to let their minds wander into innovative places.

People whose brains are largely STRUCTURAL will likely need to know that no one will take it personally if they hold the team to the agenda and to the topic at hand.

People whose brains are largely SOCIAL will likely need a safe space in which to express their emotions about the topic and not be judged.

E

A

People in the first third of EXPRESSIVENESS will likely need to know they will be left alone until they are ready to speak.

People in the third third of EXPRESSIVENESS will likely need to know they can speak freely.

People in the first third of ASSERTIVENESS will likely prefer a minimum amount of drama.

People in the third third of ASSERTIVENESS will likely need to know they can debate without hurting anybody's feelings.

People in the first third of FLEXIBILITY will likely need to be certain that the purpose of the meeting will not change.

People in the third third of FLEXIBILITY will likely need to feel they will not be forced to pick a solution until they are ready.

Important Note: None of these attributes stand alone, but rather thread together in a way that produces WEteam magic.

Principle #5

USING THE POWER OF WE

*Techniques to Unleash Your
Team's Potential*

There is a great deal you can do on your own to ensure that Emergenetics principles filter down into every corner of your company, like water reaching the roots of your organization, if you learn how to apply what we call the *Power of WE*. This principle describes the practical application to do this.

WHO IS YOUR FAVORITE CHILD?

Think about your company's goals. If you have written them down somewhere, don't look. Take out, or draw, a blank Emergenetics Template. (There is one at the end of this chapter for you to copy.) Label each area of the template. Do not worry about dividing the spectrums of the behavioral attributes into thirds – just use **Expressiveness**, Assertiveness, and Flexibility.

Now go find other people who will remember the company's goals, such as your administrative assistant, or the operations manager, or the vice president of human resources. Ask them if you left out anything. If you are like most CEOs, you probably did. We tend to remember those goals that pique our own thinking and behavioral attributes. You may have left out something that is not immediately important to you, but it might be very important to your employees, or your customers, or your company.

Congratulations! You just learned something about how your brain works, and you also used the Power of We. Of course, you could have just looked at your list, but this way you can link the real people who caught your missing goals to other ways of thinking and behaving.

HELP! I DON'T HAVE A PERFECT WEteam!

To unleash your organization's potential, there is nothing like the creative tension that occurs between the different Emergenetics attributes to spark innovation and productivity. The optimum way to release the Power of WE is to form a perfect WEteam, as explained in Principle #4. If, as a group, you have represented all the thinking attributes, plus, you have a mix of first-third, second-third, and third-third behaviors, *and* you have a trimodal or quadramodal thinker, then you have created a bona fide WEteam that is ready to work (provided the team has a clear goal, mutual respect, and trust). If any of the attributes are not represented, you will need to take what we call a WEapproach, which is a catchall term for taking an inventive way to create the effect of a WEteam even if you don't have one.

The following three emergency measures will ensure you have a WEteam result, even if you don't have a perfect WEteam. A wonderful byproduct of these approaches is that they all call attention to the strengths of every attribute. Everybody is expected to emulate each attribute, whether they possess it or not. This fosters belonging, embraces diversity, permits divergent viewpoints, builds mutual respect, and encourages transparency and honesty from the top down as well as from the bottom up.

EMERGENCY MEASURE #1: INVITE AN OUTSIDER TO JOIN YOU

The easiest way to fill the gap in your WEteam is to invite someone who has the missing attribute to join you. Someone else in your office surely can help. If this person already is familiar with the goal of the team, that's a bonus – but it's not absolutely necessary. Share your project and invite this individual's perspective. Even if your new team member is from another division, or another profession altogether, providing your team with the missing attribute will produce insights that your group would not otherwise have considered.

EMERGENCY MEASURE #2: THE EMPTY CHAIR

If the members of your WEteam are familiar with Emergenetics, they will already have a good understanding of all the attributes, whether they personally have them or not. When an attribute is missing in a team, all the members can endeavor to be more aware of the different energies present in the room and make a conscious effort to consider the perspective of all attributes, including the missing one.

One great technique for covering all your bases is called the *Empty Chair.* If you almost have a complete WEteam and you need to remember the perspective of a particular attribute, give it a chair at your table. No, I mean it – give that attribute a physical seat at your table. Pull up an extra chair and in some manner (a sticky note, a label on a piece of paper, a sweater that's the same color of a thinking attribute) show what attribute this chair represents.

After you have brought up your separate chair for the missing attribute, be sure to occasionally stop and invite its perspective. This simple technique will make a big difference. In order to contribute from the point of view of the missing attribute, team members will have to flex their innate preferences and step outside the ways in which they normally think and behave. Initially this is scratchy, but representing the missing viewpoint *always* is beneficial to the meeting. It also benefits your own brain. When you begin to practice this technique and work on building in areas that are outside of your comfort zone, big things happen. You build new neural pathways, stretch your way of looking at the world, and find that it gets just a little bit easier to relate to others who aren't like you. You're better able to relate to and adapt to the needs of business partners, clients, and customers, which can only have a positive impact on your business, and ultimately on your bottom line.

EMERGENCY MEASURE #3: WEboarding

WEboarding is another simple process that works beautifully when you need to be sure every attribute has its moment in the sun. Here's how you do it:

1. Get ten large sheets of flipchart paper and post them around your meeting space. Note that you need ten sheets of paper,

not seven. That is because this exercise includes both the first-third and third-third ends of the behavioral attributes.

2. On each chart write the name of one attribute:
   Analytical
   Structural
   Social
   Conceptual
   First-third Expressive
   Third-third Expressive
   First-third Assertive
   Third-third Assertive
   First-third Flexibility
   Third-third Flexibility

   You do not need to make charts for the second third or It Depends groups.

3. Now give the team members time to move about the room and quietly capture their thoughts about what each attribute would add regarding your topic. Have them write at least one insight on every piece of paper, whether they have that attribute or not. The idea is to flex attributes, not to retreat into the familiar. I usually allow at least ten minutes for this process, although more time is needed for larger groups.

4. Read all the responses and review them as a group. Determine what to do with all the information.

Let's say you are designing a marketing plan for your company, and you have put up all the pieces of paper for each attribute. What would the **Analytical**, Structural, **Social**, and Conceptual brains want to know? What messages would appeal to these parts of the brain? What resonates with first-third and third-third **Expressiveness**, Assertiveness, and Flexibility?

One of the great things about WEboarding is that you cover every essential aspect of your topic in one go-around. Each step you take during your meeting is forward progress, with very little backtracking and spiraling. WEboarding keeps the momentum always moving forward.

USING A BLANK TEMPLATE

A blank template is extremely useful. It provides a space for each attribute's priorities and concerns on a one-page worksheet.

When you need feedback on a particular idea, circulate a template to your personal WEteam. Maybe you want to solicit ideas from others but don't want to call a meeting or interrupt their work. Hand them a description of your issue with a blank template and say something like, "I need some brainstorming on this topic. Can you please write some ideas for as many of the attributes as you can, and return this to me later?"

We do this all the time in my office, and it's a particularly good way of reaching people in the first third of **Expressiveness** because they need time to process their thoughts. People who are very private may not want you to see that they write using a ruler or that they heavily rely on spellcheck. They just want to be able to safely write down their contribution in their office and get it back to you.

Other ways to use a blank template include:

- Use it to prepare for a sales call, regardless of the Profile of the person or people to whom you will be speaking. You can brainstorm your pitch, making sure you're hitting the different attributes, have thought through different scenarios, and have an Emergenetics-based answer for anything that is thrown at you.
- Take it to a meeting and privately jot down what you hear to make sure the discussion is hitting all the attributes.
- Note things you want to say for upcoming parts of the conversation so you don't forget.
- Use it to have each attribute signed off at the end of a project.
- Refer to it when preparing a presentation to remind yourself how to appeal to all the attributes.
- Use it when crafting a mission statement.
- Use it when outlining curricula or team-learning exercises.
- Consult it when you prepare a performance review to ensure you're not letting your personal biases get in the way.
- Consult it when you're creating marketing messages to make sure you are addressing all your customers.

Just keep a blank template in your pocket or inside your notes and you'll find more ways that it fits in your life – even your personal life. Brainstorm how to renovate your house, write a new book, create a holiday card… the possibilities are endless! The end result is a more creative and productive solution in much less time.

EMERGENETICS® TEMPLATE

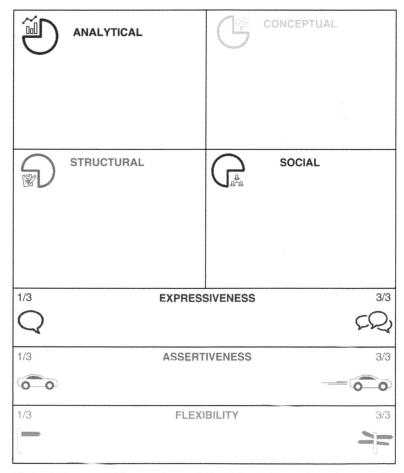

Note: We use this version of the blank Template internally to circulate through our offices.

In order to create a brand new training program, the operations department used our blank template to make sure they covered all the bases and took care of all the details that sometimes get lost in explaining and putting to use a new program. Using WEboarding – so everyone considered the concerns linked to every attribute – they generated all the questions they would need to address before and during the new program. The blank areas on the template helped them to not only organize their responsibilities but also anticipate the thoughts and behaviors of the clients so they were prepared for any eventuality. I'm inserting a copy of the Operations Program Template at the end of this chapter so you can see how this process works for us. You may want to use the same questions when you're vetting a project, or you may need to refine these questions and add some of your own.

WHAT'S THE RETURN ON INVESTMENT (ROI) IN A WEapproach?

I've spent all this time talking about WEteams and a WEapproach and *how* you can access the Power of WE, but I feel like it's also important to cover *why* you should employ these techniques.

First of all, a WEteam and the WEapproach have a direct impact on your bottom line. One global research and consulting organization determined that successful collaboration in teams drives improved company performance. They surveyed 946 global decision makers with key positions in a range of industries, including financial services, government, technology, and healthcare. These leaders were associated with companies that had annual revenues ranging from $U.S. 5 million to over $U.S. 10 billion. They were asked questions about collaboration within their organizations. The study found that not only does collaboration affect profitability, sales growth, product development, customer satisfaction, and innovation, but effective collaboration is *the* most important indicator of a company's overall performance. Another study found that 75% of business executives rank collaboration with vendors and partners as a top priority. And it's not necessary to reinvent the wheel because by adapting the successful ideas of others you can leverage their ideas using your own creativity and productivity. And the best way you can ensure effective collaboration is by using WEteams and a WEapproach.

SUCCESS AT WYNDHAM VACATION OWNERSHIP

Wyndham Vacation Ownership (WVO) is the world's largest vacation ownership business, with over 219 resorts as of this writing. WVO also is a long-term user and implementer of the Emergenetics Profile, and one of the first organizations I worked with that is an example of Emergineering.

After experiencing a tremendous amount of growth, WVO was faced with the challenge of relocating its company headquarters to make room for all of the new employees they had hired, plus those they were planning to hire for future growth. The undertaking required a multimillion-dollar renovation of a 25,000-square-foot building in Orlando, Florida. To take on a project of this magnitude, WVO needed to assemble a high-performing project team that included representatives from many departments and levels of the organization. In addition to internal team members, there also were vendors and contractors to coordinate with the project's goals, budget, and timelines. The development of the new building and relocation of employees needed to be well coordinated and seamless in order not to disrupt productivity and business operations. So how did WVO go about such a massive undertaking – one that would take nearly a year to complete? They Emergineered it.

The project team of more than 25 internal leaders, as well as external vendors and contractors, completed an Emergenetics Profile. As part of the project kickoff, the group participated in a teambuilding Emergenetics workshop to help people understand their own Profiles as well as the Profiles of others on the team. Then they used smaller WEteams as needed to help them communicate more effectively, manage conflict, and come up with innovative solutions for the challenges they faced. The Emergenetics Profile became an essential resource for communication, task completion, and process development from beginning to end.

The results were outstanding. The WVO corporate headquarters were relocated not only within budget but also early – two things that nearly are unheard of with a project of this size. It took only 11 months to complete, which had a significant impact on the company's bottom line. Not only that, but there were new ideas that arose from the creative tension of the project development

WEteam, including new design concepts never seen before at WVO, which employees loved.

PUTTING IT ALL TOGETHER: A WEteam MEETING WITH AN EMPTY CHAIR

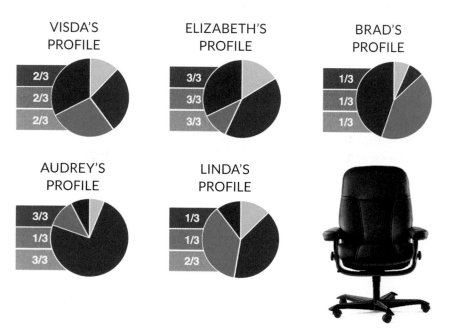

A small but important group of people had reserved the conference room at our headquarters for meetings, two half days in a row. A large transportation company that had already received some Emergenetics training wanted to take Emergenetics principles deeper into their organization. They had just signed on for a full year of Emergineering. Three of our Emergenetics employees, along with two associates from the other company, had eight hours to create an individualized plan. The team had a lot of ground to cover – and they had never even met face-to-face.

The agenda for day one was to create a smoothly functioning team, clarify where the company wanted to ramp up its Emergenetics strengths, determine how we could best provide support for them in those specific areas, and brainstorm how to Emergineer their entire workplace culture – plus show how we ultimately would help their bottom line. The agenda for day two was to determine exactly what needed to happen when, who would be responsible for what, how success would be measured, and so on. The objective was to walk away on day two with a concrete plan of action for the entire upcoming year.

As you no doubt have experienced, meetings in which the participants don't know each other can take a long time to get up to speed. Everyone wants to be polite, and at the same time they are trying to evaluate everyone else. Is there an obvious authority figure? An idea person? A stonewaller? Someone who will not talk? Someone who won't stop talking? Is it safe to venture an opinion, or is this just a meeting to rubber stamp what the boss already wants while pretending to be inclusive? The team members from Emergenetics had some techniques to offer that would make this meeting both productive and efficient. In turn, the two associates could take these techniques back to their company and use them in their meetings.

The bad news was that there was not much time for pleasantries or teambuilding exercises. The good news, however, is that everyone had the one thing that would help the team move swiftly from competing to completing: an Emergenetics Profile.

Everybody already had seen their own Profiles, except for one of the participants, Elizabeth, from the transportation company. Fortunately, she had heard enough discussions about Emergenetics that she had the general idea. She just didn't know her specific Profile.

Visda, meeting chairman, spoke first. She handed Elizabeth her Profile and said, "Congratulations! You're an **Analytical/Social** thinker!" Elizabeth immediately turned to Audrey, her partner from the transportation company, to share her Profile.

"See?" explained Audrey. "You are in the third third of **Expressiveness**, the third third in **Assertiveness**, and in the second third in **Flexibility**."

Audrey showed her Profile to Visda. "I'm a single dominant **Social**, and all of my behaviors are third third."

Visda said, "Well, Elizabeth, you probably have a lot of questions about exactly how your percentages and percentiles were worked out, right? What the science is behind all these nice colors?"

Elizabeth looked surprised. "Well, yes," she admitted. "I mean, I know it's accurate because I trust Emergenetics, but these numbers are so precise. I see here I'm way over at 95% for Assertiveness. Does that mean I'm a pain in the neck?"

Visda laughed. "No, no! We don't use negative terms like that. But you probably like a fast pace and don't mind debating your point of view. I'm guessing you're the kind of person who likes to drive fast and can't stand having slow people in front of you."

"That's interesting!" said Elizabeth. "My husband complains about my driving all the time!" The rest of the team laughed.

Next, Visda asked everyone to hold up their Profiles. People always enjoy seeing how their Profiles contrast with those of others, but most importantly it's extremely helpful to see each other's strengths and to note things like who needs quiet time to recharge, who needs to wiggle around, who will not be interested in details, who will vacuum them up, and so on. The team would have another chance to see each other's Profiles shortly, but this was a great way to break the ice. Elizabeth laughed when she found two buddies at the other end of the Assertiveness spectrum. "I think I'm getting this," she said, studying her Profile some more.

Next, Visda introduced the 3-2-1 Exercise:

3. Share three things the team should know about your leadership style.
2. Share two points about your Profile that you need to be aware of when working with others.
1. Explain how you would (or would not) prefer to be spoken to or communicated with, and tell us what role or responsibility you would like to have in this meeting.

Visda went first. She had a multi-modal brain – **Analytical**/**Structural**/**Social** – and her behaviors were third-third **Expressiveness**, third-third **Assertiveness**, and second-third Flexibility. She could easily communicate with each person in the room and became the translator for the group.

Visda's preference for Structural thinking indicated she was time-sensitive and interested in concluding their task not only perfectly but also on deadline. She said, "I'm going to live in my Green, and keep us on track. I'm not going to apologize for my Assertive-ness because I want us to drive to a conclusion that we all agree is successful." Visda made it clear up front that no one should be offended if she said, "We need to keep this moving." She had to be able to push for deadlines, commitments, and alignment without being perceived as harsh. The team *needed* her to drive everyone forward. This was established as a norm at the outset, so every-one would respond appropriately when Visda had to refocus the discussion by saying "Let's move on," or, "I haven't heard a timeline on that."

All of the team members took turns explaining what they wanted the others to know about them in a team setting. All meet-ings have competing interests and personalities, but viewing them in terms of Emergenetics removes the fear factor. The quiet, stoic team members explained that even if their expressions did not change and they didn't say anything, they really were listening; they actually did have opinions; and they would prefer not to be put on the spot about them until they were ready to talk. Others explained that they needed data as well as logistical information before reaching a decision. If they pushed for all the facts, this was in no way meant as an accusation. The team members went around the table, sharing their 3-2-1 information.

Elizabeth went last. "Now I see why I'm so logical," she said, "and people either love me or hate me on airplanes because I can talk to them for the whole trip – unless they put in their earbuds. I'm guessing that's my combination of a Social brain with this third-third Expressiveness. As for communicating with me… there *is* no wrong way to communicate with me!"

In another situation, Elizabeth might be regarded as a showoff, but here it was clear her outgoing personality and forcefulness were simply her nature. Emergenetics creates an objectivity about the way people think and behave by showing how individuals are innately wired to react. Provided you have a group that has good intentions – which this group did – Emergenetics removes the sub-jective aspect of verbal and nonverbal communication that can hurt feelings, spark tempers, or even destroy progress altogether. Usually when a meeting is not going well, people question each other's motives, can't see eye to eye, and don't feel understood or appreciated. They get cranky; cooperation goes out the window; and they start working independently or in smaller groups. Here, team cooperation was a top priority. Nothing was taken personally because everything was interpreted in terms of Profiles.

All the attributes of all the team members had their moment to shine, and the entire exercise took only 15 minutes. Almost immediately, they sensed a candid, trusting atmosphere developing among each other. Already they could feel the healthy, creative tension and synergy that occurs when collaborating team members have diverse ways of thinking and behaving.

Next, Visda posted all five Profiles on the wall as a reminder of the perspectives each person was bringing to the table. The Profiles were there to be used as a reference and reminder throughout the meeting. With them on the wall, a team member could point and say, "I'm living in my **Blue** right now," or, "we've been pretty **Red** for the last 30 minutes – let's bring it into the **Green** a little bit and put some structure around these ideas," or "let's get **Green** for a few minutes and establish commitments around these ideas rather than just having good ideas."

As they posted the Profiles, Visda noticed there was no bona fide preference from the Conceptual tribe:

"OK, then," said Visda. "This is the perfect time to use the Empty Chair." She pulled an extra conference room chair up to the table. Audrey said, "Look! I'm being Conceptual already!" She had taken a piece of computer paper and drawn a yellow smiley face on it with curly hair to represent the missing Conceptual brain. "I want to name him Edison."

Visda wrote EDISON under the smiley face and taped it to the chair to remind everybody to flex their Conceptual attribute as the meeting went on. She said, "The Conceptual neurological pathways bring innovation and new ideas to the discussion. People with Conceptual thinking can look at things upside down or from other points of view and see possibilities other people do not. They also think big – the big picture, the long term, how everything fits together on a grand scale. Without a Conceptual attribute on this team, we will do a great job putting together a practical timeline, but we also might overlook a creative solution." Visda asked everyone to occasionally make sure the Conceptual attribute was receiving enough attention. The team members would flex outside their usual attributes and contribute the way Edison would contribute.

To Elizabeth, this felt very scratchy, and because of her Profile, she had to comment on it. "You really need a chair?" she said skeptically. "Is it that important?"

The Emergenetics people all started talking at once, assuring her that yes, it was that important. Visda explained, "When we use this technique, we don't just invite Edison to the table. We flex our own attributes, and become more skillful at thinking and behaving outside our comfort zone. Actually, it's not easy. We will have to pause every now and then and switch to the Edison point of view. However, you should know that for you and for your company, this builds new neural pathways in our brains, and in turn that makes it easier for us to relate to colleagues, clients, customers, and others who are not like us. At Emergenetics, we've found that this creates a better corporate climate for everyone."

Visda changed the subject. "I need to mention a few housekeeping details that will help keep this meeting on track. We have a small group, so I don't anticipate any problems, but there are a few things to keep in mind. As I mentioned to Elizabeth, at Emergenetics we avoid negative terms. We believe that every attribute brings something important to the table, so before you get annoyed with others, look at their Profiles on the wall and determine where they are coming from. If you have any personal biases – and most of us do, whether we acknowledge them or not – leave them at the door. This is a safe space in which to throw out ideas. You should feel free to be yourself – just be yourself politely."

The team members smiled. They all could remember meetings where things got impolite.

The company associates did a quick review of the company's mission and financial health. The overall outlook for the company was mixed. Their branding was satisfactory for the time being and their business had good consumer recognition. But they were in a very competitive field. The more difficult times got, the harder it was to keep a competitive edge.

For years, the company had been spending enormous amounts of money on technology without thinking much about employees.

The new CEO realized that a company is only as good as its workers and its workplace culture, and was willing to invest in people. There was too much dissatisfaction, too much turnover, and he had no patience for putting out fires between competing executives. There was real work to be done. He picked Emergenetics because he realized that the colors were easy to remember and the Profiles were easy to understand, at least on the surface. This was an approach that would work for everyone at every level.

Audrey and Elizabeth offered to answer any questions the team members from Emergenetics had. What cost-cutting measures was the company taking that they should know about? What could this company do that others could not? In what ways did they want to distinguish themselves? Exactly how did they measure success? What was the corporate culture like? What were their offices like?

Someone who had been thinking about transportation in general had an Edison moment and said, "I hear they are bringing back blimps!" At first this comment didn't seem to add much to the discussion, but then the team began to discuss what transportation was going to look like three, five, or ten years ahead. How could this company position itself to be on the vanguard?

There were many good questions, but Visda reeled the team back in and pushed for specific needs. First, the company wanted to integrate Emergenetics into all aspects of its training and development programs. Some diversity training was needed as well. These were straightforward tasks that Emergenetics handles all the time for many kinds of companies. The biggest questions were with whom, and how often? The details were set aside for further discussion.

The company wanted to use Emergenetics to create a collaborative corporate environment that reached every single worker. They wanted to make working for their company a good experience and retain more of the employees they trained. The associates handed out an Emergenetics report that listed every employee they had from the CEO down to the newest intern.

Linda, the third team member from Emergenetics, who had first-third **Expressiveness**, piped up and said, "I was wondering if you have sent out any surveys? And if so, who received them; what kind of questions did you ask; and what was the feedback?" No, they had not sent out any surveys. The previous CEO was not interested in feedback. "The absolutely best option is to get Profiles for *all* the employees!" burst out Audrey. Then she added, "Edison has a question. Everyone here – except me – is familiar with the Emergenetics+ smartphone app. Could we use that somehow to reach everyone? What if we entered everyone from our company in your database? Could you distribute surveys that way? Or could we collect the employee self-tests and compare them the way the app compares actual Profiles?"

"Good idea," Brad said. "If we put everyone's profile on the app everyone can communicate with each other in the same language, even though they live in different cities and countries."

The team persevered, with a break after two hours to let the quiet members recharge and active members go outside. Everyone also had a brain-boosting snack to prevent meeting fatigue. By the end of four hours, they had a clear idea of what Emergenetics could provide for the company, plus some questions to discuss the next day. This break also gave the quieter members of the team time to digest their thoughts so they would have brilliant things to contribute the next day.

On day two, Visda opened by saying, "We don't want to leave here just all happy fuzzy warm. We need to spell out where the company is now so we can measure our success later. Then we need a specific timeline of what we will provide and when. Would anyone like to start?"

Visda continued to act as a connector the whole time. She could bring in a **Red** story, or bring in a **Blue** analysis, or bring in **Green** by asking, "How can we make sure we don't lose that idea?" or "What can do to make sure that does *not* happen?" Brad was **Blue/Green**, whereas Audrey was single dominant **Red**, but Visda could bring those brains together and make sure the team still was on track.

Brad wanted to know the latest about the transportation company equipment, hardware, and software. What shiny new things were they using? What was coming?

This led to a discussion about freebies – things the company could give away to remind employees about Emergenetics every day. These had to be inexpensive but effective.

"What about decks of cards? It could have your logo on it."

"That sounds expensive. Plus, you *know* there would be cards all over the floor."

"What about food? Everybody likes food."

"Yeah… but I bet people would be concerned about food allergies, or they would be on a diet."

"How about travel-size soaps and things, like the ones in hotels?"

"I dunno about that. I already have my favorite shampoo; I don't need another."

"You know, I still have pens in my house from my electrician, my insurance agent – even my dentist. What about pens?"

This time there were no objections. Everybody needs pens. They could be distributed everywhere in the company offices. Or all the employees could get their own. Anything that happened in writing could be a reminder of Emergenetics.

"Edison is back!" exclaimed someone. "What if each pen is a different color, and has some kind of statement on it? Like the **Blue** pen could say 'Bring me data!' "

The team brainstormed different sayings, and everything went swiftly until they got to **Red**.

"Here's a good one!" said Audrey, the **Social** company representative. "How about, *'For penning heartfelt memories?'* "

"Oh BLECHHHH!" someone burst out. The rest of the team members looked up in shock.

"Well, that was heartfelt," said Visda dryly.

"I'm sorry," Brad quickly apologized. This behavior was unheard of for Brad, a first-third **Assertive**. "That just came out. But can't we focus on a different aspect of **Social** thinking? Like telling stories?"

Everyone else in the room who had **Red** in their brains started talking at once. They were practically standing up. "Oh no, that's perfect! We have to have that, that's the best one of all of them!"

"Brad!" said Audrey. "How could you *say* that?" Her **Social** attribute was taking this discussion personally.

Brad was still having a visceral reaction to "heartfelt memories." To him it sounded sappy and stupid, but he quickly recovered his first-third behaviors. He tried to frame his response a little more diplomatically. "Personally, I would never pick up this pen."

The **Red** brains in the room were unmoved. "Well, we would pick up that pen *first*," they argued.

Brad put up his hands in surrender. "OK, I recognize that I have a **Blue**/**Green** brain and I just don't get it. I can accept that everyone else jumping around the room is proof that this **Red** statement is a good one. I am not the expert, so I should not be providing feedback for this particular discussion." In the end, Brad was willing to go with "heartfelt memories" not because he liked it but because he had proof that the appropriate brains did.

The team was so effective in hitting its objectives that it created a timeline and rollout schedule, including some contingency planning, before the eight hours of meeting time were up. This was an incredible achievement. When the meeting ended, Elizabeth and Audrey, in their reflections, said, "We wish all meetings could be like this!"

REFLECTION

Think of all the experts studying meetings and leadership and empowerment whose research has not made any difference. Business books are like diet books – everybody reads the latest one, but nothing changes. That's why it's time for WORK THAT WORKS!

It's staggering to think that millions of meetings are taking place all around the world every minute of the day. Think of all the styrofoam cups of coffee on conference tables, the PowerPoint presentations, the office politics, and the anger, frustration, humiliation, and shame with which people leave their meetings. When it comes to people, things inherently get complicated. Think of the time wasted!

Now, although you may never have experienced one, reflect on how much of that nonsense you could eliminate by using a WEteam. Everyone at the meeting is present because they are competent, have a common goal, and have ideas to contribute. When it is appropriate, invite the head of customer care to inform you how your products are doing, or the head of warehouse returns to show you which items are coming back due to poor workmanship, or the head of delivery to explain why trucking expenses are so high. You need information from the front lines.

Make sure the Language of Grace is used and the room is a safe place to speak for all of the attributes. When you can see the rubric of thinking and behavioral attributes that explains how an individual would approach something, or want to be approached, this suddenly makes human interactions more objective. Conflict, change, and projects all can be discussed swiftly and productively in terms of Profile. Conversation flows; ideas quickly come to fruition; things happen in an almost effortless way. When you integrate a WEapproach into everything that your company does – from on-the-job training, to creating productive working environments, to revising your corporate culture, to how you structure your meetings – it will improve your outcomes and you *will* see results. The energy that you put toward always using a WEteam or WEapproach will show in your profits, and your bottom line will thank you for it.

IMPLEMENTATION STEPS

1. Check your hiring procedures. Do you have systems in place that ensure you are hiring for both competence (see Principle #4: Meeting of the Minds) and cognitive diversity?

2. Get Profiles for your team. Do an Emergenetics analysis of the group. Are any attributes missing? Over-represented? Under-represented? Are all the best brains at the table? Use Emergenetics attributes to create project teams instead of rank and role. The right attributes and skills will create cross-functional WEteams. If you don't want to start a conflagration by taking out a weak link, at least you can invite new competent people to join you.

3. If necessary, use one of the three Emergency Measures as a WE approach.

TEMPLATES FOR PRINCIPLE #5:
THE POWER OF WE

1. HOW WILL DIFFERENT MINDS READ THIS BOOK?
   People with different thinking and behavioral attributes will approach this book differently.

2. THE OPERATIONS PROGRAM
   The operations team used the template to brainstorm a newly developed operations program. First, they came up with questions for each attribute that they needed to address before they had finished the project.

3. EMERGENETICS TEMPLATE

How Will Different Minds Read This Book?

People with different Thinking and Behavioral Preferences will approach this book differently.

F

A reader with a majority of ANALYTICAL thinking will appreciate the proven scientific data and research behind the ideas in this book.

A reader with a majority of CONCEPTUAL thinking will flip through this book looking for some of the more *cosmic woo-woo* ideas.

A reader with a majority of STRUCTURAL thinking will read this book from front to back, looking for practical tips and applications.

A reader with a majority of SOCIAL thinking will enjoy the case histories about real people in real business situations.

E

A

Readers in the first third of EXPRESSIVENESS will reflect quietly on the implications of this material.

Readers in the third third of EXPRESSIVENESS will want to share something interesting.

Readers in the first third of ASSERTIVENESS will check to see if the ideas in this book are non-confrontational.

Readers in the third third of ASSERTIVENESS will want to determine their preferences as soon as possible so they can read this book quickly and efficiently.

Readers in the first third of FLEXIBILITY will look for evidence that it is worth committing themselves to the ideas in this book.

Readers in the third third of FLEXIBILITY will be intrigued by the *cosmic woo-woo* information in this book.

Important Note: None of these attributes stand alone, but rather thread together in a way that produces WEteam magic.

The Operations Program

The Operations Team used the Template to brainstorm a newly developed Operations Program. First, they came up with questions for each attribute that they needed to address before they had finished the project.

F

The ANALYTICAL brain may ask: "What are the objectives and solutions? What's the ROI? What's the value of doing this program? What shall we charge? How will we measure success?"

The CONCEPTUAL brain may ask: "Are there any other things we haven't considered? How do we make this program attractive and unique? How does this relate to other programs?"

The STRUCTURAL brain may ask: "Have roles and responsibilities been assigned? What materials do we need? Do we have a project management system and a timeline for the development of the program? How do we implement this program?"

The SOCIAL brain may ask: "Who does this program impact? How will the experience make them feel? Who is the sponsor of the program? Are key roles defined? Is there anyone else we need to involve on the team?"

E

A

People in the first third of EXPRESSIVENESS will likely ask: "How can we promote the program via email? How much of this program is self-guided?"

People in the third third of EXPRESSIVENESS will likely ask: "How can we promote the program in person? How much of this program is group-based?"

People in the first third of ASSERTIVENESS will likely ask: "What is a comfortable pace to move at in order to implement this program?"

People in the third third of ASSERTIVENESS will likely ask: "How quickly can we get this going?"

People in the first third of FLEXIBILITY will likely ask: "Is this program mandatory?"

People in the third third of FLEXIBILITY will likely ask: "Are we open to new ideas or a new pathway?"

Important Note: None of these attributes stand alone, but rather thread together in a way that produces WEteam magic.

EMERGENETICS® TEMPLATE

ANALYTICAL	CONCEPTUAL
STRUCTURAL	**SOCIAL**

1/3	**EXPRESSIVENESS**	3/3

1/3	**ASSERTIVENESS**	3/3

1/3	FLEXIBILITY	3/3

Principle #6

LET YOUR PEOPLE LIVE TO WORK, NOT WORK TO LIVE

A Job Is More Than the Time Between Vacations

Attitudes toward work have changed dramatically since the old days when people put in 50 years working for the same utility company and were rewarded with a gold watch. Loyalty has undergone a seismic shift. Employers today continue to be surprised by "those millennials," but when you look at how they were raised and the world they inherited from previous generations, their behavior really is not surprising at all. I wanted to find out how the different generations answered questions about their work/life balance, as well as getting, keeping, and valuing a job.

TWO GENERATIONS: CHANGING ATTITUDES TOWARDS WORK

I started with a member of Generation X. He now has grown children, so he has been in the workforce since before the days of office casual and calling your boss Frank instead of Mr. Melancholy.

THE OLDER GENERATION SPEAKS

You have no doubt heard of life hacks, like shortcuts for your cell phone, the fastest way to fold a t-shirt, or ingenious ways to use ice cube trays. Ken, a 50-year-old man who works at a credit card processor company for financial institutions, is a genius at work hacks. He finds ways to fit good times into his job without getting fired.

> "My company was doing a reduction in force (RIF), so my boss told me to take my scheduled vacation to Mexico but to check in every hour. I made an agreement with my assistant that she would send me a text at the first hour, and I would answer her in the next hour. She would text the letter A, and another hour later I would text the letter B. On the second day, she would text the number 1, and an hour later I would respond with the number 2. Then I would not

hear from her again for another hour. Because we were in the same time zone, I got two hours of unlimited vacation time – and when I went back to work, my job was saved because I had a record that I had communicated with the company every hour on my vacation!"

Ken used technology to beat the system. Can you guess his Emergenetics Profile? He continues:

"Recently I was in Colorado hunting bighorn sheep. I took both my camping gear and my business attire because in the middle of the week I had to leave the mountains for two days, fly to Cincinnati, and make a presentation. Then I returned to the mountains."

"Isn't that a lot of stress while you are on vacation?" I queried.

"That's the way it is!" he responded. "I do this because I am a good corporate citizen, and I am inured to the pain this may cause me or my family. A millennial would say, 'Can't we figure out another way to cover my work so I can take my trip?' It never even occurs to me to ask the question. Putting in the time is part of the job description. This is the deal I have with the corporation. The millennials who I know won't take a job if they don't like the dress code. When I was looking for a job, this would have never occurred to me."

"Well, Ken," I asked. "Surely you could have figured out another way to cover yourself and stay on vacation? I believe this is about how much power you are willing to exert. Research says you can go out further than you think from your manager's expectations before you get fired."

"That's right," he said. "I would not have lost my job, but I would have lost political capital."

I said, "The principle I am interviewing you about concerns work/life balance. What do you say about that?"

"I come from a generation that still believes in the company, and naively so. The corporation used to take care of us, but these days companies are connected into profits and Wall Street and not connected to the employee. I don't think badly of them. My loyalty doesn't lie with the company but with my desire to learn and get into my next position. My generation is a dying breed. My children and their generation don't care about what the company wants. Look at how we raised them and how school treated them. Why would we expect them to behave differently in their jobs?"

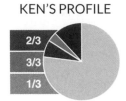

KEN'S PROFILE

2/3

3/3

1/3

A MILLENNIAL SPEAKS

I wanted to find out from a real live millennial if this was all true, so I had a conversation with Abby, a 23-year-old we hired at Emergenetics straight out of college for her first job.

ABBY'S PROFILE

2/3

2/3

2/3

I asked, "Abby, what were you thinking about as you were applying for your first job?"

She replied, "I asked, 'What do I value, what does my company value, where can I make an impact, and how am I making a difference in someone's life?' When I can answer all of these in a positive way, I feel energized, dedicated, motivated, and productive. If I can't answer these questions, I wonder what's the point, why am I here, could I be doing more good somewhere else, and am I valued?

The way people job search, find their role, and design their career path is changing. Increasingly, the individual's purpose, their passion, and their connection to their work are being brought to the forefront. People are asking themselves 'What is my purpose as a person, how can I connect to this in the most meaningful way, who can I affect while I help to create a better life for me, and where can I find meaning and be valued for who I am?' Salaries and security are no longer priorities. If there is no connection to the company, the role, or the people, the desire to stay leaves. Connecting employees to their purpose and making them feel valued and empowered will lead to higher retention rates.

Abby shared, the purpose of life is no longer simply to sustain yourself. Jobs and money will come and go. The priority is to have a purpose with no regrets. People are starting to value the intangibles. Each person's passion and idea of making a difference is going to be different. Mine just so happens to be sustainability and social responsibility on a global level. My brother is making a creative and innovative product in an existing industry. My best friend is making sure that all animals are well cared for and taken care of by means of marketing services and products. We all are just looking to find our place and make sure that some of our life goals are being accomplished, and if that can be through our jobs, that would be ideal."

FOUR GENERATIONS

There are four different generations in the workplace today, and each one (with some overlap in between) is characterized by different personalities and different expectations of work and a working environment. Very simply, these generations are as follows:

1. *The silent (also-called traditional) generation,* parents of the baby boomers. This generation is smallest. Their cohort tends to be very loyal to one company and to remain there for their entire careers.
2. *The baby boomers.* Their cohort tends to be driven by the accumulation of wealth and the financial success that a career brings.
3. *Generation X.* Their cohort likes to maintain a work/life balance. When X'ers come to the office, they like to concentrate on work. When at home, they like to concentrate on the family. There is very little blending of the two.
4. *The millennials.* Their cohort believes that work should be an extension of home. They view the office as a living space, a source of long-term friendships. They are driven by a company's purpose more than by a compensation package.

How you approach work is constantly updated, influenced, and modified by the events that you share with your generation. Ken, an X'er, approached his vacation with the mindset of ensuring that he stays a "good corporate citizen." Abby, a millennial, is greatly energized by the positive impact that she is having on the world.

As Andy Krupski puts it, "A purpose-driven brand is not only focused on its competitive advantage in the marketplace, but also how it impacts the world in which it operates and how they treat their employees. Today brands, institutions, and governments alike need to stand for more than just the pursuit of profit. They must be visionary, with a view to being relevant over time by playing a positive role in the world. This path is the only way to build *trust*, a key and fundamental variable that drives profitable growth. All of this must be created in an environment of total and constant transparency of the vision and goals, and the plans and actions designed to meet these goals."

DO YOU LIVE TO WORK, OR WORK TO LIVE?

When it's all over, how is a life defined? Is it important to you to make a contribution to something bigger than yourself? How do you hope people will remember you? As a loving child, spouse, partner, or parent? As a successful career breadwinner? As an inventor, a community organizer, or a steward of the Earth? All or none of the above?

Ken, above, lived most fully during his vacations. His job was the time he spent in between, earning enough money to take another vacation. He works to live.

Abby, our millennial, won't settle for anything less than an ideal job that she can be enthusiastic about every day. After finding employment in a company with a working environment she enjoys, tasks she likes doing, people she enjoys seeing, and a global cause she can endorse, she lives to work.

Living to work means being excited about heading to work in the morning. A job is energizing, people feel valued, and they feel they are part of a collective whole. They believe their contributions truly do make a difference, whatever the size of the organization. Living to work is the simple idea that you find meaning and purpose in the endeavor in which most people spend the vast majority of their waking hours.

HOW CAN YOUR COMPANY MEET THE NEEDS OF ALL GENERATIONS?

Ken and Abby have vastly different expectations of what the company is supposed to provide for them, and what their contributions should be to the company. As a leader, you must provide a space that honors these different generational perspectives and meets their expectations.

As millennials make up a larger and larger part of the work force, we have more and more of them in our office. As their numbers have increased, we have had to re-examine some of our well established processes for completing work. Do we have fair pay standards? A diverse workforce? A pleasant work environment? A system for helping employees progress? We have gotten scratchy.

At first it was frustrating to have freshly hired 20-somethings immediately ask to be part of high-level discussions, or ask if they could go home at 3:00 p.m. to give companionship to their pet. Little by little, however, we realized that they were always connected with the office by cellphone and always available to come in at some point. Their requests to take their puppy to training class, or to leave early for improv theater practice, or to go skiing because the powder is exceptional, became less threatening.

Ten years ago, I heard a futurist speaker who suggested that all businesses should hire a couple of 20-year-old employees because they have a lot of technological knowledge. He was right. When we did this, we found the climate in the office became refreshing and energetic because these new hires not only solved our annoying computer and electronic problems but also created innovative products to enhance our business.

In companies across the globe, the old-fashioned view of work is being challenged, and it doesn't seem like this will slow down anytime soon. A recent poll showed that in 2015, 62% of all new mothers were working after having children – an increase over

2005. With this increase of millennial mothers in the workforce, where there is an increasing expectation that the workplace is to resemble home, the issues have changed again. Does your office have a breastfeeding room? Do you have a generous family-leave package? Will you allow a mother to work from home?

These ideas don't just apply to women. You can't overlook young fathers. Do you have paternity leave? Do you have flexible hours so that fathers can be available for their children while their mothers work in the office? Is it acceptable for either parent to bring an infant to the office? These questions are still scratchy for us.

Emergineering your organization can create a culture that honors these different approaches to work and helps bridge the gaps between all generations. That being said, our millennials have taught some of us the important lessons of *living to work*.

HOW TO BALANCE THE PROFESSIONAL WITH THE PERSONAL ON THE JOB

Some of the practices that we have implemented in the office (regardless of generation) maintain a strong sense of professionalism while still addressing work/life balance. These include:

1. We deliver constant feedback so employees can progress toward their career goals.
2. We often order in meals to bring everyone together and bump up morale.
3. We hold exercise challenges (or some similar type of self-improvement initiative).
4. We have the expectation that workers will be available when needed and get their work done in a timely fashion.
5. We are as transparent as possible, even with sensitive financial documents.
6. We make our office an attractive place where employees will want to hang around.
7. We find ways to engage each other in a less formal, more collegial manner.

8. We often take time out to engage in discussions involving global events.
9. We solicit feedback from everyone on almost all major decisions.
10. We have an employee charitable-contribution-matching program.
11. We offer two paid days off per year during which employees can volunteer for charities they're passionate about.

Each of these policies is designed to help the well-being of all employees, engage their interest in local and global initiatives, and help them progress in their careers. When you combine these policies with a customized, Emergenetics approach to their preferences, this provides an accepting, safe environment for any generation, and any Profile, to contribute and to succeed.

We learned from Terence Quek and Deborah Chew, our CEO and COO respectively of Emergenetics Asia Pacific, that they believe the office is the second home for most of their team, and many of them spend more time in the office than at home. For that reason, they make the office a comfortable place.

Another aspect of work they find extremely important is coaching, which helps everyone progress. They do not use the U.S. mentor/student model, but a process of mutual improvement.

COACHING

Terence Quek explains:

> Across our organization, we view coaching as an integral element to strengthening our company culture and encouraging development. We use the Emergenetics Profile as the foundation of our discussions and often stop to notice how people's preferences are reflected in their work and can be used to drive their performance. This level of reflection supports an environment of feedback and continual improvement for all members of the organization. Coaching is not just for the members of our

leadership team. We provide coaching for all levels of the organization. For instance, our Emergenetics Asia Pacific office engages in a process of Collegial Coaching, a unique approach introduced to us by our Associate Ng Choon Seng.

Central to the theme of collegial coaching is the belief that anyone within the organization can coach anyone else. This is unlike traditional forms of coaching, where the coach is usually someone professionally certified, senior, or potentially external to the organization. How about being coached by anyone from the organization?

We knew it would take time and effort to integrate this into our existing culture – even though ours is already open to learning. We formed coaching pairs to practice on a regular basis. The management also intentionally invited junior members of the team to be our coaches, to demonstrate our commitment toward creating an open coaching culture within the team. Not only do I now have regular contact with a team member with whom I would otherwise have little opportunity to work, but I am also getting fresh perspectives from the ground up on how I am doing as a leader.

As a leader, it is important to be vulnerable and to be willing to embrace coaching in the right spirit. That means being humble, open to feedback, and being authentic. It may be scary initially, but the rewards are definitely worth it.

On top of the benefits of traditional coaching, collegial coaching produces more self-awareness among team members, and it shortens feedback cycles. More importantly, it builds relationships and trust, and strengthens the culture we built using Emergenetics – one that is inclusive and harnesses diversity. Also, collegial coaching cultivates a greater sense of ownership, by encouraging accountability toward the team results.

The model employed by our team in Singapore is a particularly good one to use with millennials in your workforce.

It allows for a level playing field, where open dialogue is exchanged between any two colleagues, regardless of position. It also reflects a constant measure of a company's purpose, and each individual's contribution toward that purpose.

Coaching and continual feedback are important aspects of building a productive culture, and Emergineering the process greatly enhances its overall effectiveness. Before any formal performance discussions take place, both parties share their Emergenetics Profiles and compare/contrast the similarities and the differences of the two. I would recommend that the pair intentionally devote time to discussing how each person prefers to give and receive feedback, and what the preferences say about how they would like to improve. This process can also be reinforced by the two people connecting on the Emergenetics+ app, where specific tips can help aide the understanding and effectiveness of the relationship.

If you successfully Emergineer your coaching program, you will likely see:

- A reduction in ramp-up time of participants getting to know each other. The Profile and conversations with each other will help them connect, engage, and decide on the next steps moving forward.
- Trust developing quickly between the parties, as they are better able to interpret each other's words and intentions using the Profile.
- Decisive action steps that play off of each individual's preferences.

Lastly, I would recommend that the pair often check to make sure their preferences are being honored and maximized. Emergineering is a long-term commitment to cultural improvement, and referencing these principles will provide lasting return on investment with your employees.

REFLECTION

It's clear that the business world is moving to a more open form of management – one where a company's value is seen less on a balance sheet and more in the eyes of its employees. To stay ahead of this trend, it is folly to think that the traditional separation of work and personal life will create an attractive career option for the up-and-coming generation.

Creating an environment where your people live to work will give you the competitive advantage to succeed in the future. A job is no longer simply the time you spend between vacations. As leaders, our goal is to make work meaningful, so that the Abbys and Kens of the work world live fully and happily during the dash between their birthdate and time of death. Today, talented employees want purpose and connection from their employers, and if they can't find it from us, they will seek it out from others.

IMPLEMENTATION STEPS

1. Honor the different generations:
   a. Provide a forum for genuine and safe discussion about the different generations represented within your office.
   b. Craft policies that reflect a healthy respect for the needs of each generation.
2. Provide meaningful coaching; pair up with a nontraditional coach.
3. Emergineer your conversations.

TEMPLATES FOR PRINCIPLE #6, LET YOUR PEOPLE LIVE TO WORK, NOT WORK TO LIVE

A job is more than the time between vacations.

1. Questions Millennials Can Use to Bridge the Gap with Other Generations
2. Questions to Ask Millennials About Their Work
3. How Each Attribute Prefers to Be Coached

Questions Millennials Can Use to Bridge the Gap With Other Generations

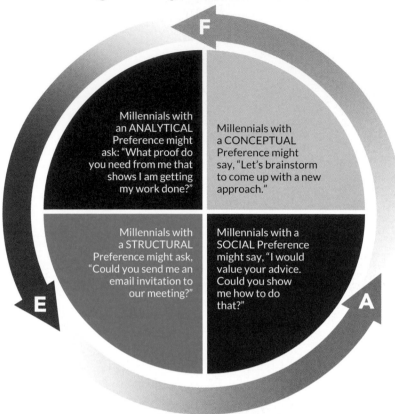

F

Millennials with an ANALYTICAL Preference might ask: "What proof do you need from me that shows I am getting my work done?"

Millennials with a CONCEPTUAL Preference might say, "Let's brainstorm to come up with a new approach."

Millennials with a STRUCTURAL Preference might ask, "Could you send me an email invitation to our meeting?"

Millennials with a SOCIAL Preference might say, "I would value your advice. Could you show me how to do that?"

E

A

Millennials in the first third of EXPRESSIVENESS might say, "I prefer to communicate electronically. I will give you my thoughts via e-mail."

Millennials in the third third of EXPRESSIVENESS might ask, "Can we talk this out?"

Millennials in the first third of ASSERTIVENESS might say, "I like to work at my own pace."

Millennials in the third third of ASSERTIVENESS might ask, "Could you give me immediate feedback on this?"

Millennials in the first third of FLEXIBILITY might say, "I can handle change, but I work better when I can trust that you will not change your mind."

Millennials in the third third of FLEXIBILITY might say, "I like things open-ended. I'm happy working in an ever-changing environment."

Important Note: None of these attributes stand alone, but rather thread together in a way that produces WEteam magic.

Questions To Ask Millennials About Their Work

F

Leaders whose thinking is largely ANALYTICAL might ask Millennials: "In what ways are you adding value to the company?"

Leaders whose thinking is largely CONCEPTUAL might ask Millennials: "Do you have any ideas to contribute?"

Leaders whose thinking is largely STRUCTURAL might ask Millennials: "Can I count on you even though your physical presence isn't here?"

Leaders whose thinking is largely SOCIAL might ask Millennials: "How do you prefer to socially engage with the rest of the company?"

E

A

When leaders ask Millennials in the first third of EXPRESSIVENESS "How can we effectively capture your ideas?" their answer might be "I will send you my thoughts."

When leaders ask Millennials in the third third of EXPRESSIVENESS "How can we effectively capture your ideas?" their answer might be "I will send you a text."

When leaders ask Millennials in the first third of ASSERTIVENESS "How should we meet to discuss our project?" their answer might be "Let's check in as necessary."

When leaders ask Millennials in the third third of ASSERTIVENESS "How should we meet to discuss our project?" their answer might be "Let's talk about it right now."

When leaders ask Millennials in the first third of FLEXIBILITY "What is the likelihood that you will change your approach?" their answer might be "Only if there is a compelling reason."

When leaders ask Millennials in the third third of FLEXIBILITY "What is the likelihood that you will change your approach?" their answer might be "Let's see what happens and adjust as necessary."

Important Note: None of these attributes stand alone, but rather thread together in a way that produces WEteam magic.

How Each Attribute Prefers To Be Coached

F

The ANALYTICAL Attribute might say, "Give me a fair assessment of my work and the benefits of changing."

The CONCEPTUAL Attribute might say, "Show me how my work relates to my long-term development and how I can keep my work interesting."

The STRUCTURAL Attribute might say, "Show me a step-by-step approach for improvement."

The SOCIAL Attribute might say, "Show me that you acknowledge my feelings."

E

A

Those in the first third of EXPRESSIVENESS might say, "I'll follow up via email."

Those in the third third of EXPRESSIVENESS might say, "Allow me to voice my thoughts before we reach a conclusion."

Those in the first third of ASSERTIVENESS might say, "Please be constructive."

Those in the third third of ASSERTIVENESS might say, "Give it to me straight."

Those in the first third of FLEXIBILITY might say, "Explain to me how making this change is important."

Those in the third third of FLEXIBILITY might say, "I'd like to consider all the possibilities and circumstances."

Important Note: None of these attributes stand alone, but rather thread together in a way that produces WEteam magic.

Principle #7

LOVE

Care for Your People and the Profits Will Come

Let me start by saying the word so seldom uttered in the corridors of business: LOVE.

See? Nothing bad happened.

I am *not* talking about office romance, or your love of God and country, or your family love, or even how much you love your dog. I am referring to leadership love.

As a leader, you know what it feels like to have stewardship over people who depend on you, and look up to you, and to whom you owe your success. If you really cannot stand anyone who works for you, you should get a new job because you cannot succeed alone. Your organization will not thrive without your attention and love.

I am in charge of a successful business. I am fortunate. I worked hard. But I am not superior to my employees. Because of my relationship with them, they are better people and I am a better person. We both grow. My promise to them is that I will be honest, kind, encouraging, supportive, and uplifting. Sometimes our relationship will hurt. I may give them constructive feedback, but they will be better for it, and I will be better for it because I will not have compromised my integrity by looking the other way.

I experience leadership love for my workers. I see their familiar faces and know I am in the right place. They see me and have confidence that someone is in charge of our ship. This workplace love is mutual, and it is something to cultivate and treasure because it creates enthusiasm and loyalty and minimizes fear. No employee can do their best if they are afraid.

At Emergenetics, we study the *brain* and its effects on how people think and behave. But the *heart* is in everything we do. We know that we change people's lives by helping them understand their work and personal lives. We think about integrity, communication, collaboration, creativity, motivation, attitudes, teamwork, trust, problem solving, critical thinking ... those things the United States Department of Labor lists as soft skills.

Because of the nature of our work at Emergenetics, it may be easier for us to have Love as a Principle, so I asked Mary Rhinehart,

CEO of Johns Manville, if Love is a principle in her organization. Her first words were, **"Love what you do, and the profits will follow."**

The Johns Manville organization, based in Denver, Colorado, was started in 1858. It manufactures insulation, roofing materials, and other engineered products. Employees deal with tangibility, certainty, and measurability – so-called hard skills. Yet Mary loves what JM is about. As Lance Armstrong famously said, "It's not about the bike." Mary doesn't love roofing materials. She loves making things happen and seeing people thrive.

When you ask Mary about leadership love, she states that she "bleeds JM Blue." She is devoted to her work and seeks new things to learn every day. Her employees and customers all find it inspiring to see the JM workers collaborating in teams and offering genuine concern to their customers and to each other. Mary believes that JM is "making the world more successful because they are building and improving environments and energy efficiency."

Mary embodies leadership love because she is present. The first thing she did when starting her role was to bring her team together to build relationships. She showed that she valued cognitive diversity, and she also set expectations. Her employees speak glowingly about her. She believes that the success JM has experienced is because of her ability to be fully attentive to her organization.

Mary spends more time on her staff and customers than the typical CEO because she understands the importance of corporate culture. Mary calls this the *secret sauce*. She is credible, responsible, open, transparent, and results-focused. She also attributes her success to her thirst for learning and improving.

Every one of those traits is absolutely critical to success in today's business environment, and calling them soft subtly diminishes their importance. Soft skills have an image problem, and it is time to change that.

When my third son, Morgan, and his wife-to-be, Annie, were planning their wedding, I took Annie out for dinner. Because this was the third wedding in our family, I had learned a few things about integrating in-laws into our family. Starting with an intimate dinner was an important beginning! As we sat down and chatted, she asked me how it had been to welcome new family members. I paused and said, "You know, it isn't all at once. The day you marry Morgan, I feel like I will say a big yes to your relationship, but I have already been saying many yesses along the way as we have gotten to know each other. The yesses will continue, though, throughout your marriage, having children, holiday celebrations, vacations, and arguments as we deepen our relationship. It is through these regular and consistent yesses that love emerges."

My favorite analogy for love is a bold, hearty, authentic **YES**. People offer one another plenty of superficial yesses each and every day. A yes can be self-serving or a deflection or even subterfuge. Conversely, a true yes – either to a person or an organization – requires mutuality, reciprocity, and deep influence from one to another. Love primarily is a series of agreements that deepen our relationships with ourselves, others, and our world. The actions we take as a result of these yesses lead to change, growth, and greater depth of understanding.

We do not say yes all at once, and neither do we love all at once. Rather, it is through consistent, timely, and dependable acts that we build the sort of love that is true, selfless, and timeless. As a leader, you can model how to show love in all your actions, which will greatly influence not only your direct reports but also those with whom you interact on a regular basis, from the UPS driver to the barista you see each morning. Organizationally, when we focus on leadership love instead of a short-term goal, we create a workplace culture of mutual respect and affection that is greater than any specific leader, any one program, or any successful endeavor. It builds the sort of organization for which people say, "I love to work there!" and will continue to say so for generations.

Building a culture of love, however, does not begin and end with you. Your good deeds, appreciation, and warm handshakes are not enough to create a corporate culture of love. That must be built upon the shared actions through the workplace that are for and among all employees, from the C-suite to the line workers. Every level of an organization needs to be speaking and living their yesses comprehensively, consistently, and out loud.

Allison Fass, Executive Director of Digital at *Inc. magazine*, notes that seven components for 21st-century leadership are balance, empathy, genuineness, humility, inclusiveness, vulnerability, and patience. All these promote a culture of love, as do qualities like presence, gratitude, and joy.

PRESENCE

Distraction and preoccupation have become the norm rather than the exception in today's workplace, and we carry this same scattered perspective back to our homes at night. The sense of being in balance is an ever-elusive and moving target as we juggle home and work and seek to keep each one in their proper place. One gift at Emergenetics is that we empower employees to define their own work/life balance. They are in charge of how they will be present at work and at home, and we do not require them to create stiff boundaries between the two. We ask for full presence in the office instead, and have found that when people are allowed to concentrate when it best suits them, they are more efficient, on task, and productive. When we allow ourselves to be fully present and mindful of what each moment calls for, we have greater success.

At Emergenetics, when we have our weekly meeting (as I talked about in Principle #2), we become present through the practice of centering. Also, in our office, if someone needs ten minutes to walk and be present to themselves, they take it. If two individuals need to share about their weekend plans with full presence to one another, they do so. We ask that the same full presence be given to their work in return, and we have found that giving people permission to focus on both personal priorities and work makes us a better company. When we say yes to being fully present, we have the energy and attentiveness to love our work, our home life, our coworkers, and most importantly, ourselves.

One event that inspired me to write this book happened last spring. A new employee asked if she might take the afternoon off. She was visibly nervous asking this favor, but she wanted to assist her son in preparing for his first prom – getting the corsage, making sure the tuxedo was properly adjusted, taking photos. … It was no big deal on our end, but how many times does a mother have this opportunity? She was shocked that our team was sensitive to her life and her personal priorities.

We are mindful that, as much as each person in the office is our colleague, that person is also a daughter, a son, a brother, a sister, a mother, a father, a volunteer, an ardent fan, and the list goes on. If we assume that an individual belongs to us and us alone, then we are being selfish and we only hurt ourselves. And so, to be mindful of everyone's lives, we provide enough space and trust to allow individuals on the team to take a few hours off to run errands or take care of an ailing parent. When trust is given to them, each person becomes more mindful of what they need to give back to the company. Each person also knows that a colleague will cover for them if they go on leave, and vice versa. We've had a flexible leave system for 25 years, and I can safely say nobody has abused it.

GRATITUDE

The next quality only works if we master the first! Real gratitude cannot grow from chaos and insincerity. It must follow presence and understanding. When we focus on what we are truly grateful for, we shift our perspective into a place of opportunity and hope. Naturally, love follows! Communicating with gratitude invokes humility as we articulate how we have been influenced and changed by another person or by the organization. Naming our gratitudes makes us subtly vulnerable as we acknowledge to our workplace and coworkers that we are not cold, distant planets. As we say thank you, we open ourselves to receiving love, and our gratitude is multiplied by a thousand by someone who is not expecting any special recognition.

Now you might be thinking, "How am I supposed to find the time to write personal notes when I have [insert important obligations]?" You don't have to write an essay. See the template on page 168 for how to thank people in ten words or less. Use the Profiles of your employees as a guide. Thank-you notes need to be genuine and appeal to what each person values. Saying, "You're doing a great job!" is fine for people with a preference for **Social** thinking, but **Structural** thinkers won't trust you unless you add a specific task they have accomplished.

When it comes to greetings, people with a preference for **Analytical Structural** thinking often are more formal in their communication and prefer a greeting like, "Dear Ann." People with a preference for **Social** thinking will most likely be fine with an informal greeting that uses their name, such as, "Hi, Mike." People with a preference for Conceptual thinking don't require a name at all. It will not hurt their feelings if you just start with, "Greetings."

I like concluding slightly longer thank-you notes by mentioning next steps, again in a manner related to each person's Profile. For example, for your hard-charging (your third-third behavioral attributes) workers you might use, "Now is the time to hit the ground running! See you at the Bongo account meeting next Monday." For more stoic (first-third behavioral attributes) workers, you could say, "I'm very excited by how this is shaping up. With your help, the Bongo account meeting on Monday will be a big success!"

There are other things that a leader who falls in the first third of **Expressiveness** can do to create a workplace climate of gratitude. When spoken words don't come out as easily, put into place practices and space for the sharing of ideas, thoughts, and feelings that cater to each employee's preferences. For example, in the Singapore office they've got a white board where they can stick notes of appreciation and encouragement for a team member. They also allow for the exchange of cards of appreciation in their retreats twice a year. Team members put down their thoughts and feelings on paper and share them with each other. It is during these times that all individuals are reminded of how important each one is to another on the team. With these words, they empower each other, which contributes to the meaningfulness of the work we do.

In the Denver office, we have a Gratitude Jar. Anyone who wishes to add a note may do so. Once a week, we open the jar and the notes are read aloud. The people who are mentioned usually are surprised and happy, and the rest of the team is happy for them.

For the **Analytical** thinkers who believe people should simply do a good job because that's what they are paid for, keep in mind that there is a self-serving aspect to thanking people. When you recognize the contributions of others, you reinforce the kind of behavior you want to see again. When their efforts are noticed, and they know their work makes a difference, people are more likely to go the extra mile in the future. Also, most corporate cultures are so impersonal that employees are more likely to stay with you if you are kind to them. And finally, thanking people makes *you* feel good.

Notice your people and be present to what they do and who they are. Communicate your belief in them and thank them for what you see in them. Speak to where you see them growing, and honor who they are becoming. Regularly practice gratitude as a leader and in your organization, and watch a culture of love grow.

JOY

It is not uncommon for laughter to bubble throughout the halls and in our meetings at Emergenetics. And it is not the corporate polite laughter. It is the belly-shaking, childlike zeal for life! We regularly poke good-natured fun at ourselves and find plenty of opportunity to share openly in the funny stories and situations that grace our lives. We literally dance, play music, and relish in building community in the workplace. Even from our inception, we began every Emergenetics seminar with brain aerobics, and we laugh heartily at how ridiculous we know we look to the outside world. When you hold life as lightly as a feather, you find more fun (and more meaningful connections) in our interesting and ever-changing world.

Joy cannot exist without sorrow, so we also cry together. We are not immune to the pain and grief that touches our lives, and we share grief and hold space with one another. We do not rush in with advice and quick fixes when difficult times arise but stay the course with one another in our personal and collective challenges.

Because we embrace life's experiences so fully, joy finds us time and time again. And a culture of love is a culture of joy.

Kelly leads the ESP (Emergenetics Selection Program) in our Denver office. She is a bright and cherished teammate who is a senior leader in our company. Kelly discovered that she had developed a rare form of cancer. She began chemotherapy as a result and continued to welcome our office in sharing her journey and story. In these moments with Kelly, life seemed very unfair and unjust and we lamented with her the pain she experienced.

At the end of her chemo treatment, Kelly and a few coworkers proposed that she host a lemons-to-lemonade party to invite joy into her experience. She reflected later about her party. "I honestly don't know how to thank everyone for such an amazing chemo party! Every smile and hug (for me, and between all of our friends) made my heart burst! We had a great night of chaos – remembering chemo moments, playing games, making bright yellow chemo drinks, playing with the pups, enjoying the food everyone brought, and so many laughs. ... This chemo party was EXACTLY what I needed. It made the most delicious lemonade out of all of those lemons."

Joy is action. When we choose to find delight in our world and say yes to the goodness in life, love follows. In our office, we celebrate often, and we celebrate what may seem inconsequential to some but is profound to us. We celebrate milestone achievements along our way, no matter where they come from in the organization. Celebrating sales is common in organizations, and although we certainly celebrate sales at Emergenetics, we actively seek out life and joy in all areas of the organization to honor, no matter where it originates.

We have a regular rotation of interns at Emergenetics. It can be easy to minimize these relationships as temporary and shallow, but we celebrate the opportunity of young minds and hands eager to help us out! We had an intern this year who was on her college basketball team. Shari, her supervisor, was fully present with her, listened to her, was grateful for her contributions to the organization and sought to celebrate the joy in her life. She organized a basketball night out for the office to go see her play, complete with fun signs to cheer her on (and maybe embarrass her!). The basketball night out was such a moment of joy for the office that many people bought a series of tickets to go see her play regularly. I like to think that our gratitude for this young woman permeated her life with love, just as it infused our organization with affection and joy.

Of course, joy is not just throwing parties and going to basketball games. Rather, joy is finding delight in our human experience. When we can find delight in the small moments, like sun streaming through our office window, the sense of completion at the end of a project, discovering just the right solution for a complex problem, or receiving a thoughtful email from a coworker, joy abounds and grows. When we are present to the joys in our workplace and celebrate them, we love where we are, what we do, and who we are with each and every workday.

BOUNDARIES AND ACCOUNTABILITY

Whereas authentic love is true, fluid, and spacious, there also is a point when the graduating levels of yes reach a place where we need to say no. Even with a corporate culture of love, a business must be run like a business or it will dissolve. Joy allows us to jump from star to star, but there is not enough time in the day to manage each person's illness, divorce, aged parent, or other consuming need. It's important to understand that when love is no longer reciprocal, what is most loving is to say no.

Understanding when to say no to an individual or an organization comes from recognizing the root of our no. Are we being selfish? Fearful? Proud? Or do we sense a genuine commitment to preserve and maintain the values, culture, and mission of the company?

Leaders daily need to determine to what and to whom they will say no. Denying employees' requests or needs on a regular basis damages trust, undermines credibility, and reinforces rigidity. Eventually, employees stop asking for assistance or will circumvent leaders to get their needs met organizationally. Good leaders regularly ask themselves how to balance love and accountability without pitting the two against each another.

One of the core values of Emergenetics is family. It can be a challenge to put our words into actions. In particular, in our rapidly growing business we often struggle with how to enact our value of treating our associates, employees, partners, and clients like family. We aim to approach each individual with the platinum rule (treat others as they would like to be treated) instead of exclusively focusing on profits or deliverables. We care about what happens after business hours. We know our associates beyond their contract. We value the business journey we are on, knowing that financial gain will follow.

At times, we must treat others more as colleagues and less as family for the sake of our business. There are moments when we must protect our culture, our product, or our values. Relationships can become strained or severed. We make progress and find resolution for them in these difficult interactions. We see the balance between the difficult accountability decisions and acts of love as a polarity to manage rather than a hard line to draw on one end or the other. Rather than a pendulum that swings too far from one extreme to the other, we continue to use self-awareness and company awareness to be cognizant of when we need to shift to one direction or the other.

Accountable love begins by considering a yes or a no pragmatically. Is the budget request ethical? Does the request for a meeting fit into in my schedule? Do we have the resources to manage another project? However, our fabric of presence, gratitude, and joy provides another way to consider how accountable love can be implemented organizationally.

When a yes or a no doesn't roll off of our tongues, then what is most loving? Does the budget request promote presence, joy, and gratitude? How about another meeting? What about additional resources? Weighing decisions in light of a culture of love provides a different lens for accountability.

One of the most challenging moments of accountability is the case of terminating employment. It is a struggle for all leaders to consider whether the decision to let someone go is fair and justified. On a surface level, when there are easy markers like performance, competence, or ethics on the line, the decision comes much more quickly. When the reason is more nebulous, or particularly when the individual is likeable and popular in the office, it can be more challenging to come to a quick decision.

In the case of accountable love, one approach toward these tough questions is to ask: Is this individual present? Are they bringing gratitude into the workplace? Are they promoting joy in their work? If the answer to any of these is no, it may be a moment to consider a termination from the lens of cultural fit rather than competence.

LOVE IS A VERB

I have no doubt that people have pondered the mystery that is love forever. One definition I've heard is that love is caring more for the well-being of another person than for your own. This kind of love varies from small gestures such as the gift of a flower in a cup to dramatic rescues such as the mother who pushes her child out of the way of an oncoming car. Love is not only something you *feel*; it is something you *do*. If you, as a leader, put into action all the recommendations in this book, you'll not only change the lives of your employees immeasurably – you'll change your own. As an added bonus, your corporate climate will become more energized, positive, and productive because you won't be treading water any more.

REFLECTION

Go back to the YES and hard and soft skills and love your employees. Although everyone in your organization has different responsibilities and salaries, you're all riding on the same train, and each person's efforts help everyone else's. Inspire your employees. Show them what they need to do, show them how to measure whether they are meeting their goals, and give them the tools and resources they need to succeed. But most of all: live in the truth of who you are, be present, show gratitude, and experience joy. Once you know who you are, there is no other way to be. To be otherwise is to lack integrity. When you do the right thing, life lines up, and life and work works.

IMPLEMENTATION STEPS

1. Be self-aware, authentic, vulnerable, and comfortable with yourself.
2. Walk the halls. Communicate without being defensive or angry. Answer questions with transparency. Be fully present when you talk to everyone.
3. Think about what each individual employee enjoys doing and is good at. Find out the name of the person who cleans your office.

TEMPLATES FOR PRINCIPLE #7: LOVE

1. HOW TO THANK SOMEONE THEIR WAY IN TEN WORDS OR LESS
   Saying thank you
2. TRUST BUILDERS
   What can you do to build trust with different attributes?
3. WHAT DOES LOVE MEAN TO EACH ATTRIBUTE?
   Love is a many-splendored thing.

What Does Love Mean To
Each Emergenetics Attribute?

Love is a many-splendored thing.

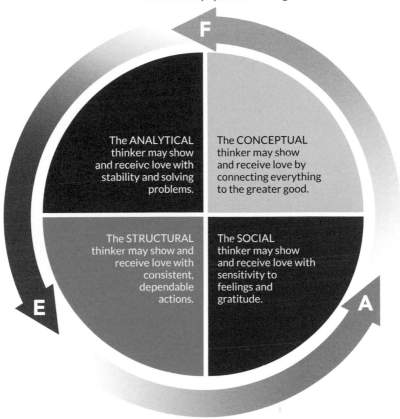

F

The ANALYTICAL thinker may show and receive love with stability and solving problems.

The CONCEPTUAL thinker may show and receive love by connecting everything to the greater good.

The STRUCTURAL thinker may show and receive love with consistent, dependable actions.

The SOCIAL thinker may show and receive love with sensitivity to feelings and gratitude.

E

A

A person in the first third of EXPRESSIVENESS may show and receive love by communicating with gentle, soft words.

A person in the third third of EXPRESSIVENESS may show and receive love with affection and ebullient words.

A person in the first third of ASSERTIVENESS may show and receive love with patience.

A person in the third third of ASSERTIVENESS may show and receive love by making things happen.

A person in the first third of FLEXIBILITY may show and receive love by giving someone all of their focus and attention.

A person in the third third of FLEXIBILITY may show and receive love by accommodating the wants and needs of others.

Important Note: None of these attributes stand alone, but rather thread together in a way that produces WEteam magic.

How To Thank Someone Their Way In 10 Words Or Less

Saying "thank you."

F

ANALYTICAL thinkers may prefer individual (not team) recognition. You might say, "I appreciate your questions" or " I respect the depth of your knowledge."

CONCEPTUAL thinkers may want to feel unique. You might say, "I value your unusual ideas" or "Your solution to the Bongo problem was stunning."

STRUCTURAL thinkers may want detailed, specific appreciation. You might say, "Thank you for perfectly transferring all that data" or "I'm impressed that you always meet your deadlines."

SOCIAL thinkers may want to please you. You might say, "I am so grateful for your team-building skills" or "I couldn't have done it without you."

E

A

Those in the first third of EXPRESSIVENESS may want you to send them an email. You might write, "I appreciate your well-considered solutions" or "I prize your respectful attitude toward everyone."

Those in the third third of EXPRESSIVENESS may desire public recognition. You might say, "Thanks for keeping the lines of communication open!" or "I appreciate how you share your enthusiasm!"

Those in the first third of ASSERTIVENESS likely want everyone to get along. You might say, "Thank you for helping to keep the peace" or "I treasure your amiability more than you know."

Those in the third third of ASSERTIVENESS may appreciate a prompt response from you. You might say, "Thank you for keeping the momentum going!" or "I appreciate your decisive action."

Those in the first third of FLEXIBILITY may have strong opinions. You might say, "I depend on your support" or "I value you for your convictions."

Those in the third third of FLEXIBILITY may not get flustered easily. You might say, "I recognize your adaptability" or "I appreciate that you take interruptions in your stride."

Important Note: None of these attributes stand alone, but rather thread together in a way that produces WEteam magic.

Trust Builders

What can you do to build trust with different attributes?

F

You can build trust with the ANALYTICAL Attribute by researching topics in advance, using the best facts and data from credible sources to support your arguments and providing value for time spent.

You can build trust with the CONCEPTUAL Attribute by providing a safe space for offering new ideas, allowing different solutions to be explored, finding value in unusual suggestions and sharing an interest in a vision for the future.

You can build trust with the STRUCTURAL Attribute by creating realistic timelines and adhering to them, following guidelines, valuing the process of reaching a conclusion and paying attention to organization and details.

You can build trust with the SOCIAL Attribute by valuing relationships, appreciating that there are feelings and emotions associated with the topic and remembering to consider the impact of any solution on people.

E

A

You can build trust with those in the first third of EXPRESSIVENESS by listening intently, giving them time and space to think and providing details in writing.

You can build trust with those in the third third of EXPRESSIVENESS by saying what you think, allowing them to talk to you and providing verbal confirmation.

You can build trust with those in the first third of ASSERTIVENESS by having people work together in a friendly manner, building consensus and calmly mediating conflicts.

You can build trust with those in the third third of EXPRESSIVENESS by saying direct responses, not taking things personally and letting them make their points.

You can build trust with those in the first third of FLEXIBILITY by explaining the reasons for any changes, following through on what you say and relying on them to stick to their decision.

You can build trust with those in the third third of FLEXIBILITY by being accommodationg, being open to new ideas and appreciating their willingness to tolerate changes and interruptions.

Important Note: None of these attributes stand alone, but rather thread together in a way that produces WEteam magic.

CONCLUSION AND ACKNOWLEDGMENTS

As I wrote the ending, I realized this book is not only a description of Emergineering but a true example of its application as well. It turns out Emergineering is so customary in our office that we subconsciously apply it to everything we do. Each chapter of this book was written with the principles in mind, and each principle was fully evident in our office as we worked feverishly to the end using WEteams (see Principle #4). Here is how I assembled our Denver employees to help me create the outline for *Work That Works*.

First, I assembled them for an hour and a half of their time. We brainstormed all the things about our office that we prize. Everybody had a chance to add their ideas. Each person had a sticky note pad, and each person wrote down, one note at a time, all *work that works* in our office. We ended up with more than 200 notes!

Second, three people took all the notes and grouped them into what finally became the seven principles. The most interesting conversation was about the *Love Principle*. Some thought it was too touchy-feely for a business book, whereas others argued that this is what we experience in our office. Ultimately, we agreed that love is an essential aspect of work, regardless how touchy-feely it seems.

Third, I organized the WEteams and gave each group one of the seven principles and one hour to design an outline for each principle that included a paragraph describing the principle, a story to accompany it, the ROI, three implementation steps, and a suggested template.

The next day, we spent another hour as each group made a presentation about their principle and solicited feedback. Bingo—in two and a half hours the beginning of this book came alive.

These employees are:
Kerry Anderson, Shari Biesboer, Linda Bontrager, Shana Bosler, Debbie Brown, Morgan Browning, Meghan Bush, Kellie Carroll, Julie Clukies, Mary Cook, Alyssa Evans, Céline Fischer, Kelly Fullerton, Jeff Gingrich, Jeneen Hartshorne, Brad Hoffman, Karen Hulett, Linda Jares, Nikki Korkowski, Annie Lengacher Browning, Katie Lindauer, Stephanie Medley, Abby Medved, Michael Miller, Caitlin Murphy, Betsy Orton, Liz Palizzi, Adrienne Quilliam, Melissa Ress, Heath Schmalzried, Sharon Taylor, Marie Unger, Jerry Van Leuven, Kelli VanderPal, Chance Villarreal, and Herm Weaver.

Later, we asked our APAC and EMEA office to add their thoughts:
Deborah Chew, Linda Ashley Chua, Ashley Devers, Sinead Devlin, Frank Diamond, Chelsea Dillon, Justin Koh, Amos Lim, Imee Anra Lim, Mark Lim, Lini Lingam, Samantha Low, Jan Ng, Dorothy Oh, Alvin Peh, Terence Quek, Naweera Sidik, Cheryl Tang, and Colin Yeow.

But they are not the only "family members" to whom I am grateful: Wendell Williams, Ph.D., my colleague, friend, and brilliant industrial psychologist.

Chris Cox, Scott Halford, Marty Lassen, Harold Suire, my first Associates; and Mary Case, MD, Neuropathologist, who keeps us updated on the latest neurological research.

Josh Teo, entrepreneur, who initiated Emergenetics Asia.

Our Advisory board: Armistead Browning, Robb Caseria, Andy Krupski, Annette Quintina, and Steve Yocum, who keep us on track.

Global partners:
Steve Bentley, Georgeta Dendrino, Bassem Emad, Ferruccio Fiordispini, Salvador Garza, Masanori Kagawa, Sangeeta Kaur, Geraldine Koempel, Nattavut Kulnides, Chris Lam, Siddharta Moersjid, Shinya Nakao, Bridgit Parise, Herve Roy, David Sales, Maria Santos, Hyuen Jeong Seo, Tieu Yen Trinh, Deanna Werklund, and Andre Wiringa.

Our Master Associates:
Shana Bosler, Rita Bouwens, Kellie Carroll, Chris Cox, Alyssa Evans, Ferruccio Fiordispini, Kelly Fullerton, Salvador Garza, Masanori Kagawa, Geraldine Koempel, Diane Lujan, Yasuhiko Nakamura, Shinya Nakao, Yumiko Nishi, Kohichi Okamoto, Bridgit Parise, Deborah Peterson, Terence Quek, Kelvin Redd, Hervé Roy, David Sales, Samantha Sales, Maria Santos, Hyuen Jeong Seo, Donna Simonetta, Harold Suire, Sharon Taylor, Oleta Tam, Josh Teo, Marie Unger, and Colin Yeow.

The colleagues, clients, and employees who gave their names and their anecdotes to illustrate these principles.

Our clients from many organizations and countries who have brought us in to Emergineer their companies. We enjoy serving them, and they teach us at the same time we are teaching them.

And most important:
Nellie Sabin, gifted editor, who tirelessly acts as a muse, friend, and intelligent guide. Without her, this book would not exist.

Tom Fishburne, clever marketoonist, and a man I am proud to call my nephew.

Key contributors were Kerry Anderson, Annie Lengacher Browning, Deborah Chew, Mary Cook, Joanne Leclair, Katie Lindauer, John Nelson, Erin Peereboom, Melissa Ress, Sharon Taylor, and Kelli VanderPal.

Denise Marcil and Anne Marie O'Farrell, agents, who believe in our work and push us forward.

Jeanenne Ray, who approached us and encouraged us to work with the creative Wiley team, which includes the brilliant brains of Tessa Allen and Peter Knox.

The people who bring special joy to my life: Rebecca, Annie, Karen, John Armistead, Willis, Holden, Emily, Nathan, Lewis, Reuben, Emmett, Lexi, and Margot Browning, Don Browning, Barbara Browning, Betty Burke, Glenda Crouch, Len Crouch, Harriette Fishburne,

Cary Fishburne, Judy Girardot, Andy Girardot, Mary Gay Gordon, Connie Graham, Andy Graham, Barbara Grogan, Bob Hancock, Elizabeth Holtze, Steve Holtze, Carol Hunter, Jane Gilbert Johnson, Eddie Johnson, Christy Miller, Carol Kingery Nelson, John Nelson, Mary Jo Rodeno, Tom Rodeno, Fran Root, Emmet Root, Tim Rouse, June Schorr, and Paul Schorr.

As I look at this impressive list of impressive people, I am reminded again that we are all connected, and that all of us are greater than some of us. My wish for you is that you will Emergineer your way into a place of such gratitude and humility. This would be my goal for your organization as you use WORK THAT WORKS!

APPENDIX

DETERMINING YOUR THINKING AND BEHAVIORAL ATTRIBUTES AT A GLANCE

Select all the words below that best describe you. You may select few or many. Select only words that identify your preferences. As you circle more words in a certain area, this is a clue that you may have a preference in this area. If you select an equal number of words from the left (first-third) and right (third-third) ends of a Behavioral Attribute spectrum, you probably fall in the It Depends group.

ANALYTICAL	CONCEPTUAL
Reasoned	Inventive
Rational	Original
Intellectual	Innovative
Objective	Imaginative
Follows logical thinking	Intuitive about ideas
Questioning	Global
Critical thinker	Unconventional
Investigative	Seeks change
Inquiring	Bored easily

STRUCTURAL	SOCIAL
Detailed	Sensitive
Disciplined	Giving
Methodical	Friendly
Rule follower	Supportive
Follows process	Intuitive about people
Organized	Compassionate
Traditional	Caring
Predictable	Empathic
Practical	Feeling

EXPRESSIVENESS

1/3   **EXPRESSIVENESS**   3/3

Avoids spotlight	Calm			Chatty
Introverted	Reserved		Talkative	Outgoing
One-on-one	Prefers safety	It Depends	Performer	Lively
Keeps feelings	Alone		Seeks attention	Extroverted
private	Quiet		Talks to strangers	Gregarious

ASSERTIVENESS

1/3   **ASSERTIVENESS**   3/3

Compliant	Accepting		Tough	Determined
Peacekeeper	Deliberate		Powerful	Competitive
Pacifier	Passive	It Depends	Telling	Aggressive
Winning isn't everything	Amiable		Forceful	Driving
Avoids confrontation				Ready for action

FLEXIBILITY

1/3   **FLEXIBILITY**   3/3

Focused	Strong opinions		Genial	Accommodating
Firm	Dislikes change		Easygoing	Changeable
Absolute	Decides easily	It Depends	Adaptable	Supportive
Narrows options	Impatient		Affable	Handles ambiguity
Prefers defined situations				Sees many options

TOUR OF THE PROFILES

Think, for a moment, that one **Expressiveness** spectrum in theory has 100 different set points, or percentiles, to describe the ebullience of all the different people in the world. Now imagine all the different permutations you can make when you add all the percentiles for **Assertiveness** and Flexibility. By now your brain should be exploding, but we aren't done. Add all the different levels of the four Thinking Attributes, and you end up with an unimaginable number of ways in which the Thinking and Behavioral Attributes thread together. That's the beauty of Emergenetics: it provides a unique way to describe *anyone*.

For the moment, let's simplify this idea and deal only with Thinking Preferences, which range from 1 to 4. Everybody has at least one Thinking Preference. Forget the Behavioral Attributes, because they immediately become overwhelming.

The Thinking Preferences can be combined and recombined in 15 different ways, starting with people who have one Thinking Preference, and ending with those people who have four Thinking Preferences. The Tour of the Profiles has examples of these 15 types of brains. The Behavioral Preferences were chosen at random to allow you to see how thinking and behavior are in reality always connected.

UNIMODAL PROFILES

These Profile types are very rare in our database — four different thinking styles account for 10% of our population. The Thinking Preferences are very predictable, as their main source of energy around their thinking comes from just one preference. In these samples, each person will act differently based on their behaviors.

Roger McDonald

Roger is a *natural skeptic* and in times of high emotion may tend to be more rational. Roger's motto may be "In God we trust...all others must bring data." While quiet, he may flex his assertive style and flexibility depending on the situation. (1% of the population)

Peter Edwards

Peter's brilliance may be in *processes, tactics,* and *operations.* Peter's motto may be "Of course I don't look busy, I did it right the first time." He appears quiet and focused and doesn't draw attention to himself. (6% of population)

Cheryl Jones

To Cheryl, how a person *feels* is almost as empirical as fact. Cheryl's motto may be "I am intuitively aware of those around me." She can swing to any one of the first-third or third-third behavioral attributes, depending on the situation. (1% of population)

Jeff Stone

Jeff's *ideas* literally pop into his head, and he tends to think in the *future.* Jeff's motto might be "I feel like I'm diagonally parked in a parallel universe." He makes a decision, and then once made will stick with the decision. (2% of population)

BIMODAL PROFILES

There are six different styles of bimodal Profiles. Each has two preferences that work in concert to make decisions and navigate through one's world. These are the most common category of the thinking set, representing 51% of the population.

Kimberly Jackson

Kimberly is a convergent thinker — *focused* in *data* and implementation of *task*. Kimberly's motto may be "Make a plan and follow it." She prefers a quieter environment, she will flex her assertive style and flexibility depending on the situation. (13% of population)

Brenda Roane and Juan Garcia

Brenda and Juan are both divergent thinkers — energized in the *big picture* and motivating *people*. Brenda and Juan may have the motto "Let's create this together." Brenda is gregarious with a driving style, and she typically prefers to go with the flow, while Juan is much more reserved and prefers a quiet serene environment. (12% of population)

Brian Robins

Brian is an abstract thinker — he prefers the *30,000 foot view* when considering decisions and seeks to know the vision and high level facts/data. Brian's motto may be "I see the forest and want others to count the trees." How he behaves will depend on the situation. (13% of population)

Vivian Tan

Vivian is a concrete thinker – she wants to *be very clear* what you want *done* and *with whom*. Vivian's motto may be "I'd love to share the experience with you, but please make an appointment first." She will lean toward a more gregarious style, is generally a peacekeeper, and is one who can keep several things going at once. (14% of population)

John Carter

John may enjoy *interpreting data* while *collaborating* with others. He is largely a talkative, external processor who enjoys a peaceful environment and is willing to go with the flow. John's motto may be "An info rmed head with a warm heart." (3% of population)

Jane Williams

Jane is a *visionary implementer*. How she behaves depends on the situation. Jane's motto may be "I make the impossible possible." (2% of population)

TRIMODAL AND QUADRAMODAL PROFILES

Those with three or four preferences are energized by facilitating in groups as they understand many sides to the story. They may also be challenged by the "committee meeting in their heads" as they make decisions. 30% of the population have a trimodal or quadramodal Profile.

Malik James

Malik is a *task implementer* who prefers working with *others*. Malik's motto may be "Efficiency with feeling." He generally prefers a quiet, amiable environment where he can focus on completing one task at a time. (7% of population)

Fred Simpson

Fred prefers *ideas* that are *strategically* aligned with *others*. Fred's motto may be "What do you think of this global idea?" He is largely a talkative, external processor who enjoys a peaceful environment and is willing to go with the flow. (12% of population)

Angela Hernandez

Angela enjoys *puzzling* through new *ideas* as she *implements*. Angela's motto may be "Ideas are for doing." She is largely quiet, yet she is forceful and focused when she has made a decision. (5% of population)

Janet Walker

Janet is an *implementer* of new *ideas*. Janet's motto may be "Creative thinking with controlled emotions." She is largely a talkative, external processor who enjoys a peaceful environment and is willing to go with the flow. (5% of population)

Barbara Burke and David Burke

Barbara and David both tend to be engaged in *every topic* with the *same energy* as others would in their thinking preference, and are good at seeing all points of view. Barbara and David's motto may be "Fair and balanced." Both can typically talk to anyone in her/his language. David's behaviors tend to the third-third so he appears to expend more energy, and if the two of them walk into the room you are probably going to notice David first. (Less than 1% of population)

HOW BEHAVIORS CONNECT TO THE THINKING ATTRIBUTES

*Using Kimberly Jackson as an example, the nuances of each Profile become apparent when we combine each Profile type with the varying sets of Behaviors. Here are six profiles of Kimberly Jackson who has a Convergent (**Analytical**/Structural) Thinking Profile, but who may be expected to vary in her interactions with others by virtue of her Behavioral results. This process of linking the Profile type with different sets of Behaviors reinforces the premise that Thinking and Behavioral Attributes do not necessarily match each other according to stereotype.*

Kimberly Jackson

Kimberly is a convergent thinker — *focused* in *data* and the implementation of a *task*. She prefers a quieter, peaceful environment and is firm in her decisions.

Kimberly Jackson

Kimberly is a convergent thinker — *focused* in *data* and the implementation of a *task*. Kimberly's motto may be "Make a plan and follow it." She prefers a quieter, peaceful environment; she will flex her assertive style and flexibility depending on the situation.

Kimberly Jackson

Kimberly is a convergent thinker — *focused* in *data* and the implementation of a *task*. She prefers a quiet environment and is driven to accomplish tasks, once she has decided on the process.

Kimberly Jackson

Kimberly is a convergent thinker — *focused* in *data* and the implementation of a *task*. How she behaves will depend on the situation.

Kimberly Jackson

Kimberly is a convergent thinker — *focused* in *data* and the implementation of a *task*. She is an external processor, driven by ideas and plans. She is steadfast and resolute, keeps her attention on the goal.

Kimberly Jackson

Kimberly is a convergent thinker — *focused* in *data* and the implementation of a *task*. She is an external processor, driven by ideas and copes well if changes happen, even at the last minute.

GLOSSARY OF EMERGENETICS TERMS

3-2-1 Exercise   An Emergenetics exercise that reviews the needs and strengths of an individual Profile in the context of a team.

Abstract Thinking   The type of thinking that prefers concepts and ideas. **Analytical** and Conceptual thinking are both abstract.

Behavioral Attributes: Three of the seven Emergenetics Attributes that describe the ways you might conduct yourself outwardly. They are represented in percentiles that suggest the level of energy you give to the behaviors compared to the population at large.

> **Expressiveness**   The amount of participation you show to the world around you. This is represented by a continuum from *quiet* to *gregarious.*

> Assertiveness   The style and pace with which you advance thoughts, feelings, and beliefs. This is represented by a continuum from *peacemaker* to *driving.*

> Flexibility   Your willingness to accommodate the thoughts and actions of others. Represented by a continuum from *focused* to *accommodating.*

Centering   A practice used before becoming engaged in a current task, which involves sitting in silent contemplation with feet flat on the ground for two minutes. Based on science that indicates this grounded time increases focus on a task or meeting.

Concrete Thinking   The type of thinking that prefers facts and actions. **Structural** and **Social** thinking are both concrete.

Convergent Thinking   The type of thinking that prefers things in practical, rational order. **Analytical** and **Structural** thinking are both convergent.

Cosmic "Woo-Woo" Psychobabble   Concepts and practices that may be used to benefit the overall tone and feeling of a group.

Divergent Thinking   The type of thinking that prefers intuition, emotion, and the unusual. Conceptual and **Social** thinking are both divergent.

eLearning   Modules or seminars conducted via electronic media to extend capabilities of and access to education beyond a traditional learning setting.

Emergenetics Profile   The result of taking the Emergenetics Questionnaire, the Profile indicates individual patterns of thinking and behaving.

Emergenetics Selection Profile (ESP)   Emergenetics-based psychometric instrument used for hiring.

Emergenetics Template   A document with sections for each Thinking Attribute and for each Behavioral Attribute.

Emergenetics Youth Report   The Emergenetics Profile for children ages 10–18 years.

Emergenetics+ App   A mobile app for any person with an Emergenetics Profile. Available for download on Android and iOS.

Emergineering   Using the tools and theories of Emergenetics in all parts of an organization to create a positive and productive culture.

First Thirds   Behavioral Attributes in the first third of the three respective spectrums: 0 through the 33rd percentile.

Flex   Acting outside of one's Profile to facilitate communication and work with tasks in a way that initially may feel unnatural.

Intent/Impact Gap   The difference between what someone hopes their communication will make others think or do and what others actually think or do based on that communication. Effective communication aims to reduce this gap.

It Depends   Behavioral Attributes in the second third of the three respective spectrums: the 34th percentile through the 65th. So-called because the individual's behavior largely will depend on the situation, flexing toward either end of the spectrum.

Language of Grace   Communicating deliberately using words with positive connotations to ensure an encouraging and meaningful encounter.

Leader   A person who sets a vision and motivates others toward that vision. All Emergenetics Attributes have leadership qualities.

Percentage   Used to show how the Thinking Attributes compare to each other. Any Thinking Attribute over 23% is considered a preference (see Thinking Preference).

Percentile   Used to show how your Thinking and Behavioral Attributes compare to the global population.

Pie Chart   The section of the Emergenetics Profile that represents the Thinking Attributes as percentages in comparison to each other.

Power of WE   The benefits achieved by using the power of Whole Emergenetics, also called a WEapproach.

Reflection   At the end of a meeting, the practice of looking back upon what was learned and sharing it with others.

Scratchy   The uncomfortable feeling when you are doing something outside your typical preferences or accepted culture.

STEP   Student/Teacher Emergenetics Program. The Emergenetics sister company focused on implementing Emergenetics theory in education.

Technical Report   A statistical analysis of the research and development of the Emergenetics Profile instrument. It follows the 2014 Standards for Educational and Psychological Testing. Visit www.emergenetics.com for more information.

Thinking Attributes: The four Emergenetics Attributes that describe how people think.

> **Analytical**   The thinking attribute that combines rational thought with abstract ideas (**Blue**).
>
> **Structural**   The thinking attribute that combines sequential thought with practical ideas (Green).
>
> **Social**   The thinking attribute that combines relational thought when working with/through others (**Red**).
>
> **Conceptual**   The thinking attribute that combines intuitive thought with abstract ideas (Yellow).

Thinking Preferences: A thinking attribute that is equal to or greater than 23% on the pie chart representation of the Profile.

> **Unimodal**   A Profile with a preference (23% or greater on the pie chart) in any single thinking attribute.
>
> **Bimodal**   A Profile with a preference (23% or greater on the pie chart) in any two of the thinking attributes.
>
> **Trimodal**   A Profile with a preference (23% or greater on the pie chart) in any three of the thinking attributes.
>
> **Quadramodal**   A Profile with a preference (23% or greater on the pie chart) in all four of the thinking attributes.
>
> **Multimodal**   A Profile that is Bimodal, Trimodal, or Quadramodal.

Third Thirds   Behavioral attributes in the third third of the three respective spectrums: the 66th percentile through the 100th.

WEapproach   Approaching tasks by using the Whole Emergenetics theory.

WEboarding   A practice used to ensure the inclusion of all Emergenetics Thinking and Behavioral Attributes while brainstorming a project or task.

WEteam   A Whole Emergenetics team composed of cognitively diverse members who have a preference in each Thinking Attribute and representation in a spectrum of Behavioral Attributes.

Whole Emergenetics   Abbreviated as *WE* in many Emergenetics practices. Promotes the use of all Emergenetics Attributes to ensure well-thought-out decisions and an effective working culture.

SOURCES

INTRODUCTION

Browning, G. (2005). *Emergenetics: Tap Into the New Science of Success.* (p. 255). New York, NY: HarperCollins.

Emergenetics. (2017). Home-Emergenetics International. Retrieved from https://www.emergenetics.com

Gallup. (2017). State of the American Workplace. Gallup. Retrieved June 09, 2017 from http://www.gallup.com/reports/199961/state-american-workplace-report-2017.aspx

Kiisel, T. (2013, January 30). 82 percent of people don't trust the boss to tell the truth. *Forbes.* Retrieved from https://www.forbes.com/sites/tykiisel/2013/01/30/82-percent-of-people-dont-trust-the-boss-to-tell-the-truth/#6c71a52c6025

PRINCIPLE #1

American Educational Research Association, American Psychological Association, & National Council on Measurement in Education, & Joint Committee on Standards for Educational and Psychological Testing. (2014). *Standards for educational and psychological testing.* Washington, DC: AERA.

Chapman, B., & Sisodia, R. (2015). *Everybody matters: The extraordinary power of caring for your people like family.* (p. 47). London, UK: Portfolio Penguin.

PRINCIPLE #2

Clenfield, J., & Nakamura, Y. (2017, February 13). Toshiba's nuclear reactor mess winds back to a Louisiana swamp. *Bloomberg*. Retrieved from https://www.bloomberg.com/news/articles/2017-02-13/toshiba-s-nuclear-reactor-mess-winds-back-to-a-louisiana-swamp

Dennison, P., & Dennison, G. (1992) *Brain Gym: Simple Activities for Whole Brain Learning*. Ventura, CA: Edu Kinesthetics.

Floyd, D. (2017, June 08). Who killed Sears? 50 years on the road to ruin. *Investopedia*. Retrieved June 09, 2017 from http://www.investopedia.com

Krupski, A. (2016, January 18). Success in the future is about changing the business model. LinkedIn. Retrieved June 09, 2017, from https://www.linkedin.com

Mui, C. (2012, January 18). How Kodak failed. *Forbes*. Retrieved from https://www.forbes.com/sites/chunkamui/2012/01/18/how-kodak-failed/#133872b6f27a

Toledo, R. (2015, October 08). The idea for Netflix came from $40 in late fees on an 'Apollo 13' rental. *Extreamist*. Retrieved June 09, 2017, from http://exstreamist.com/the-idea-for-netflix-came-from-40-in-late-fees-on-an-apollo-13-rental/

Wong, K. (2015, July 29). How long it takes to get back on track after a distraction. *Lifehacker*. Retrieved June 09, 2017 from http://lifehacker.com

Zak, P. The neuroscience of trust. *Harvard Business Review*. Retrieved from https://hbr.org/2017/01/the-neuroscience-of-trust

PRINCIPLE #3

Borchard, T. (2012, August 01). Words can change your brain. *Everyday Health*. Retrieved June 09, 2017, from http://www.everydayhealth.com/columns/therese-borchard-sanity-break/420/

Folkman, J. (2013, September 05). The plague of the pessimist leader: 8 tips to make you more optimistic today. *Forbes*. Retrieved from https://www.forbes.com/sites/joefolkman/2013/09/05/the-plague-of-the-pessimist-leader-8-tips-to-make-you-more-optimistic-today/#1a0dbe1a1861

Heineken. (2015). Heineken launches a moderation movement. Retrieved June 09, 2017 from http://www.theheinekencompany.com

Newberg, A., & Waldman, M. (2012, August 01). The most dangerous word in the world. *Psychology Today*. Retrieved from https://www.psychologytoday.com/blog/words-can-change-your-brain/201208/the-most-dangerous-word-in-the-world

PRINCIPLE #4

Lassila, K. (2008, January/February). A brief history of groupthink: Why two, three, or many heads aren't always better than one. *Yale Alumni Magazine*. Retrieved June 09, 2017, from https://yalealumnimagazine.com/articles/1947-a-brief-history-of-groupthink

Markman, A. (2012, March 08). It is motivating to belong to a group. *Psychology Today*. Retrieved from https://www.psychologytoday.com

Reynolds, A., & Lewis, D. (2017, March 30). Teams solve problems faster when they're more cognitively diverse. *Harvard Business Review*. Retrieved from https://hbr.org/2017/03/teams-solve-problems-faster-when-theyre-more-cognitively-diverse

Reynolds, A., & Lewis, D. op. cit.

Smith, E. E. (2013, October 29). Social connection makes a better brain. *The Atlantic*. Retrieved from https://www.theatlantic.com/health/archive/2013/10/social-connection-makes-a-better-brain/280934/

Soll, J. B., Milkman, K. L., & Payne, J. W. (2015, May). Outsmart your own biases. *Harvard Business Review.* Retrieved June 09, 2017, from https://hbr.org/2015/05/outsmart-your-own-biases

PRINCIPLE #6

Krupski, A. (2017, January 20). Brand purpose: The road to profitable & sustainable growth. LinkedIn. Retrieved June 09, 2017, from https://www.linkedin.com

Lavery, D. (2016). More mothers of young children in U.S. workforce. Population Reference Bureau. Retrieved June 09, 2017, from http://www.prb.org/Publications/Articles/2012/us-working-mothers-with-children.aspx

Strauss, W., & Howe, N. (1991). *Generations: The history of America's future, 1584 to 2069.* New York, NY: William Morrow.

PRINCIPLE #7

Society for Industrial and Organizational Psychology. Top ten workplace trends 2017. Retrieved June 09, 2017, from http://www.siop.org/article_view.aspx?article=1610

INDEX